INSTAGRAM MARKETING BLUEPRINT 2023

The Ultimate Beginners Guide

Becoming an Influencer, Gain Followers, and Boost your Business

KELLY LEE

Acknowledgment

I want to thank you for buying my book and for trusting me, sincerely... Thanks!

I hope my books help you find the right way to know, use, and growth with Instagram and Social Media Marketing!

Good Business!!

Kelly Lee

Find my books online

Kelly Lee

© Copyright 2022 by Kelly Lee
All rights reserved.

This document is geared towards providing exact and reliable information with regard to the topic and issue covered. The publication is sold with the idea that the publisher is not required to render accounting, officially permitted, or otherwise, qualified services. If advice is necessary, legal or professional, a practiced individual in the profession should be ordered.

- From a Declaration of Principles which was accepted and approved equally by a Committee of the American Bar Association and a Committee of Publishers and Associations.

In no way is it legal to reproduce, duplicate, or transmit any part of this document in either electronic means or in printed format. Recording of this publication is strictly prohibited and any storage of this document is not allowed unless with written permission from the publisher. All rights reserved. The information provided herein is stated to be truthful and consistent, in that any liability, in terms of inattention or otherwise, by any usage or abuse of any policies, processes, or directions contained within is the solitary and utter responsibility of the recipient reader. Under no circumstances will any legal responsibility or blame be held against the publisher for any reparation, damages, or monetary loss due to the information herein, either directly or indirectly.

Respective authors own all copyrights not held by the publisher.

The information herein is offered for informational purposes solely and is universal as so. The presentation of the information is without a contract or any type of guarantee assurance.
The trademarks that are used are without any consent, and the publication of the trademark is without permission or backing by the trademark owner. All trademarks and brands within this book are for clarifying purposes only and are owned by the owners themselves, not affiliated with this document.

Instagram Marketing Blueprint 2023

TABLE OF CONTENTS

INTRODUCTION 8
PART I - INSTAGRAM 9
CHAPTER 1 9
INSTALLING INSTAGRAM 9
    INSTALL INSTAGRAM 9
    USING INSTAGRAM TABS 11
    UPLOAD PHOTOS TO INSTAGRAM 13
CHAPTER 2 16
CREATE A SUCCESSFUL FAN PAGE 16
    CREATE YOUR ACCOUNT 16
    KEEP THE FAN PAGE 21
CHAPTER 3 24
USE OF HASHTAGS. 24
    ADDING HASHTAGS TO AN EXISTING PHOTO 24
    ADD HASHTAGS TO A NEW PHOTO 25
CHAPTER 4 27
PUBLISH A VIDEO 27
    ADDING VIDEOS TO YOUR PROFILE 27
    POST A VIDEO VIA INSTAGRAM STORIES 31
CHAPTER 5 34
WHEN TO POST ON INSTAGRAM 34
    WHEN SHOULD I POST ON INSTAGRAM? 35
    GOOGLE ANALYTICS FOR SOCIAL MEDIA ANALYSIS 38
CHAPTER 6 40
GET A THOUSAND FOLLOWERS 40

- Optimize your profile 40
- Involve other users 41
- Photo tags 43

CHAPTER 7 46

FIND OUT WHO IS NO LONGER FOLLOWING YOU ON INSTAGRAM 46

- Using the Instagram app 46
- Using the Instagram website 47
- Using the Follow Cop app on Android 48

CHAPTER 8 52

INSTAGRAM CONTACT 52

- Create a report from your computer 52
- Create a report from a mobile device 55
- Report a post 58
- Troubleshooting 59

CHAPTER 9 61

INSTAGRAM STORIES 61

- Instagram Stories VS Snapchat 64

PART II – INSTAGRAM BUSINESS 66

CHAPTER 10 66

MAKING MONEY WITH INSTAGRAM 66

- Create an interesting account 66
- Attract and retain followers 69
- Using affiliate marketing 72
- Sell photos 74

CHAPTER 11 77

INSTAGRAM AND BRANDS 77

- How to optimize your Instagram profile 81
- How to optimize your Instagram feed 83
- How to create an effective content marketing strategy on Instagram 85
- Tell a story 86
- Authenticity wins 87

Instagram Marketing Blueprint 2023

3 SUCCESS STORIES 88
6 IMPORTANT STEPS TO AN EFFECTIVE INSTAGRAM CONTENT PLAN. 89
WHAT IS THE RIGHT FREQUENCY TO POST ON INSTAGRAM? 91
WHAT TIME TO POST? 93
INTERACT WITH YOUR FOLLOWERS AND ENCOURAGE INTERACTIONS. 94
HOW TO MEASURE THE RESULTS OF YOUR MARKETING STRATEGY ON INSTAGRAM 96
6 QUICK AND PRACTICAL TIPS TO GROW AND INCREASE ENGAGEMENT ON INSTAGRAM .. 97
INSTAGRAM DIRECT AND THE RISE OF THE DARK SOCIAL 99

CHAPTER 12 101

12 TACTICS TO INCREASE SALES THROUGH INSTAGRAM 101

PART III – INSTAGRAM BUSINESS 2023 133

CHAPTER 13 133

11 TRENDS FOR 2023 133

CHAPTER 14 148

INSTAGRAM ADS 2023 148

WHAT IS INSTAGRAM ADS? 148
HOW TO CREATE ADS ON INSTAGRAM 152

Introduction

Instagram is an essential tool for businesses to include in their marketing strategies. The most widely used social network is a great channel to promote your business through its company profile.

In the past, businesses paid for advertising space, billboards, newspapers, colors, to TV spots.

Nowadays, to get known, you need to use the potential of the internet and social media, investing a smaller budget than traditional advertising, with which you can reach a large and targeted audience.

But why should a company use Instagram? One of the main reasons is that it is completely mobile.

And Instagram is the only social media app designed specifically for mobile devices that focuses exclusively on engaging visual content.

Without a significant presence on Instagram, businesses risk falling behind. Social media is where people search for restaurants, shops, brands, movies, and books to read. So there's a hard but true rule: "If you're not there, you don't exist".

PART I - INSTAGRAM

CHAPTER 1

INSTALLING INSTAGRAM

Instagram is a social network that allows its users to share photos. The application was launched in October 2010 by Kevin Systrom, the company's CEO, and is now available in 25 languages; it reached the top of the App Store charts just 24 hours after its release. Thanks to this application, you can share all the photos of your best experiences with friends and followers.

Install Instagram

Download the Instagram app. To do this, search for "Instagram" in your device's store (App Store on iOS and Google Play Store on Android) and then select the app from the search results.

Open Instagram. Press the app icon (which looks like a camera in many colors) on one of your device's home screens.

Create an account by clicking Sign Up at the bottom of the screen. Enter your email address, username, password, and phone number (optional but recommended). You also have the option to upload a profile photo before continuing.

In the 'About' section you can add information about yourself, including your name or personal website.

If you already have an Instagram account, you can press Sign In at the bottom of the app's login screen and enter your login details.

Find friends to follow. Once you create your account, you have the option to find friends from your contact list, Facebook account, Twitter account, or through a manual search. Note that you need to provide the app with your Facebook and Twitter login details to add friends from these platforms.

You can follow users suggested by the app by clicking 'Follow' next to their name.

When you follow a user, you can view their posts on your 'Home' page.

You can add friends to your account anytime, even after it has been created.

Press Done when you're ready to continue. The home page of your account opens, where you can see the posts of users you follow.

Using Instagram tabs

Look at the Home tab. This is the app's default page that shows the media content of the users you follow. From here, you can perform the following tasks:

Press the + icon in the upper left corner of the screen to record and post a story for all your followers to see. You need to allow Instagram to access your microphone and camera to use this feature.

Press the Delta icon in the upper right corner of the screen to view your inbox. Direct messages are displayed here.

Access the search page by clicking on the magnifying glass icon. It is located to the right of the Home tab at the bottom of the screen. From there, you can search for accounts and keywords by typing them into the search bar at the top of the screen.

Your most viewed Instagram stories are also displayed right below the search bar.

View your account activity by pressing the heart icon. You'll find it two icons away from the magnifying glass icon. All notifications from the application (likes and comments on your photos, friend requests, etc.) are displayed on your profile.

Visit your profile by clicking on the account icon. This is the person-shaped icon in the bottom right corner. On this page you can perform the following tasks:

Press the + button in the upper left corner of the screen to add friends from Facebook and your contact list.

Press the gear or ⋮ button in the upper right corner of the screen to display your Instagram options. From here you can edit your account settings and add friends or social media accounts.

Click on 'Edit profile' to the right of your profile picture to edit your name or username, add a biography or website, and change your personal information (e.g. phone number or email address).

Go back to the 'Home' tab by pressing the house icon. You will find it in the bottom left corner of the screen. If a user you follow has posted something since the last time you visited this page, the new content will automatically appear in this window.

Social media influencer

Scroll to the right to share a story with your followers. Ramin Ahmari, co-founder and CEO of FINESSE, says: "If you want to increase your follower count, use Instagram Stories to share your experiences. Instagram has a great new feature that allows you to ask questions in Stories and read your followers' responses. Take advantage of it! It will help you increase engagement and interaction with the people who follow you."

Upload photos to Instagram

Open the Instagram camera page. Press the '+' button in the middle of the bottom row of the page. From here, you can upload photos saved in your camera roll or take new photos.

View your camera options. At the bottom of the page you will see three different upload options:
Library - this option allows you to upload a photo that is already in your library.
Photo - you can take a photo using Instagram's built-in camera feature. You need to allow the app to access your camera to upload images in this way.
Video - You can record a video using Instagram's camera. You need to allow the app to access your microphone to use this feature.

Select or take a photo. If you are recording a video or taking a photo of a subject, you must press the round button at the bottom of the screen.
To select a photo already stored on your phone, press Next in the top right corner of the screen to continue.

Select a filter for your photo. You can do this at the bottom of the screen. On average, there are 11 filters available on Instagram. Their main purpose is to make otherwise mundane pictures more interesting. You also have the option to download filters for the app. Filters change the colors and

composition of your photos. For example, applying 'Moon' filter will turn your photo into a faded black and white.
You can also press Edit in the bottom right corner of the screen to change various aspects of your photos, such as brightness, contrast and texture.

Press Next. You should see the button in the upper right corner of the screen.

Add a caption to your photo. You can do this in the Write a caption box at the top of the screen.
If you want to add tags to your photo, you can do so here.

Note the other options for uploading images. Before sharing your photo, you can try the following functions:
Press Add People to tag followers in your photo.
Press Add location to add your current location to the photo description. You must allow Instagram to access the location service to use this feature.
Post your photo to Facebook, Twitter, Tumblr or Flickr by sliding the corresponding selector switch to 'On'. Before you can do this, you need to link your Instagram account to the account where you want to post the picture.

Press Share in the upper right corner of the screen. You have successfully posted your first photo on Instagram!
Tips
If you want to gain a lot of followers, try taking photos of unique subjects.

You can view your Instagram profile on your computer, but you cannot update your account or add photos. You can only do this within the app.

Warnings

Avoid sharing photos that contain personal information, especially if you haven't set your privacy settings properly. Also, do not add your home address or other personal information (such as a photo of your new driving license).

If you try to add a location to your photos, Instagram will ask you to access your phone's location service.

CHAPTER 2

CREATE A SUCCESSFUL FAN PAGE

Create your account

Determine the theme of the fan page. Before creating a fan page, you need to know exactly what theme it will be dedicated to. The most common examples are as follows:
A celebrity or public figure.
Atopic (e.g. a type of animal).
A belief (e.g. religion or philosophical tendency).

Download a profile photo. If you don't have a photo that represents the theme of your fan page, download it before you create your Instagram account so that you can use it during the initial set-up.
For example, if you want to create a fan page about Kermit the Frog, download a photo of him.

Open Instagram. Press the Instagram icon that looks like a colored camera. The program will open.
If you have already logged into your Instagram account, log out before continuing.

Press Sign In. You will see this button at the bottom of the screen. Press it and the first page to create an account will open.

Enter a phone number. Press the text box in the middle of the screen and then enter the number you want to associate with your Instagram profile.
If you prefer to sign in with an email, press the Email tab and enter your email address.

Press Next. There is a blue button at the bottom of the screen.

Enter your name and password. Write your full name and the password you want in the appropriate fields.
You should use a name that fits the theme of your fan page, not necessarily your name.

Press Next. You will see this blue button at the bottom of the screen.

Press Change username. There is a link in the middle of the page.

Choose an interesting username. In the text box in the middle of the screen, write the name you want to use for your page. This is the name other users will see when they search for your fan page, so make sure it's easy to remember, memorable and relevant to your topic.

Press on.

Don't link Instagram to Facebook. Press "Skip" and then "Skip" again when prompted.
You can always link Instagram to Facebook later if you need to.

Press Continue in the top right corner of the screen.
If you want to follow someone on this page, you can press Follow to the right of their name before continuing.

Press Add a photo. You will see this button in the middle of the screen. Press it and a menu will appear.

Select the photo you downloaded. In the menu that just appeared, press Select from Library and then select the photo you downloaded earlier.

Finish setting up your account. Press Next and then Save to finish creating your profile and access your new fan page on Instagram.
Setting up your fan page

Study the current status of your account. Press the profile picture icon titled AndroidIGprofile.png in the bottom right corner of the screen, then look at the screen. You should see your profile picture, a box for your bio, and the first picture you uploaded (the same as your profile picture).

This screen is what other users will see when they visit your profile.

Add a biography. You can do this by clicking on "Edit profile" at the top of the page and entering a short description of the topic of your fan page in the "Biography" field.
The bio is very important because it is often the first thing that explains the topic of your fan page to potential followers.
Many Instagram users update their bios with links to new content related to the topic of the fan page (e.g. a new song or a new book).

Research the topic of your fan page. Whether you have decided to dedicate your page to a topic, a particular celebrity, or a category (e.g. whales), you need to gather more information about it so that you can stay up to date.
By reporting current events or the latest information on the topic of your fan page, the page can become a source of news for fans.
If you know how much information is available, you can better assess what type of content you should upload.

Look at other fan pages on Instagram. There are probably already pages with a similar theme to yours; you shouldn't copy them, but you can use them as a source of inspiration.
The easiest way to find other fan pages is to press the search bar at the bottom of the screen and type in the name or description of your theme.

If possible, follow the official account that inspired the fan page. If you are creating a page dedicated to a public figure or celebrity, they will probably already be on Instagram. Follow them to keep up to date when they post new content. You should also follow that person on other social networks if you can.

You could also follow other fan pages, especially if your account celebrates a category rather than just one person. This way you will get an overview of the most important topics in the community.

Think about what will make your page unique. Based on what you have found out about existing fan pages on your topic or celebrity, try to find something that will make you stand out. For example, if you find that all other fan pages cover the same kind of general information, you can make your page more specific.

Find a photo to upload. Once you have optimized your fan page, you need to publish your first image. Start by finding and downloading a photo from the internet.

If you are creating a fan page on a very accessible topic (e.g. wildflowers), you can take the photo yourself.

Upload the first photo. To do this, proceed as follows in the camera roll:
- Press + at the bottom of the screen.
- Press the Library tab.
- Select a photo.

- Press Next.
- Select a filter.
- Press Next.
- Enter a caption for your photo.
- Share the print.

Keep the fan page

Set a visual style. One thing you'll notice on the most successful fan pages is that all the photos follow the same general style. This doesn't mean they all have to be the same, but there are some strategies you can follow to make sure all your content is consistent on Instagram.
Use the same filter for all photos (or don't use one).
Stick to a color scheme (e.g. use everything or upload black and white photos).

Interact with other fan pages. By interacting with the owners of other pages, you both have the opportunity to show your posts to new people and get an idea of what content you should publish.
Following other fan pages also helps you to keep up to date with the most important news on the topic.

Keep up to date with the topic your fan page is dedicated to. It is important to keep the content of your page updated with the latest news, as many followers expect to receive this information from you.

For example, if the person you have dedicated your fan page to is a singer who has just announced a new album, you should also announce this news on your page.

Talk to your followers. Users who follow your page will undoubtedly write comments, questions, and suggestions about your content; responding to them is very important because it allows you to nurture and - potentially - grow your following.
Talking to your followers is not only important to make them feel involved; it also serves to create a positive community where people who are passionate about the same topic can talk without being interrupted.
You can measure the success of a fan page by observing how community members interact with each other.

Post frequently. As with all social media, success on Instagram is often directly linked to a good average number of posts per day, especially in the first few days after creating a new page. At the very least, try to post content twice a day. Be careful not to overdo it. Posting five times a day or more might make users not want to follow you.

Don't neglect captions. Even though pictures make up the majority of your content on Instagram, you should write a caption for each post. These short sentences allow you to talk to your followers and ask them questions, plus they make your content look more professional.

Use popular hashtags. By tagging your posts, they will be easier to find for users who don't follow you. You should only use hashtags that are relevant to your post (avoid tags that aren't related to your content), but you can add as many as you like.

If the topic of your fan page inspires a hashtag, make sure you use it in as many posts as possible before it loses relevance.

If you can't access the Instagram app, you can use your computer to post content to your page in a pinch.

Copying or plagiarising the content of another fan page (or the official page of the character you inspired) is against Instagram's terms of service and may result in your account being suspended.

CHAPTER 3

USE OF HASHTAGS.

By including hashtags in the description of photos you post on Instagram, you can ensure that your account gets noticed. When other users search for specific hashtags, they will see photos that contain them - if they've been used correctly. You can hashtag a photo as soon as you take it, or if you want to edit hashtags, you can do this in your profile.

Adding hashtags to an existing photo

Open Instagram. Use the shortcut on the home screen or in the app drawer to launch the app. Make sure you update it regularly.

Open your profile. It is represented by a stylized bust; you will find it at the bottom right of the screen.

Select the photo you want to add the hashtag to. Tap on it so that it is displayed in full size.

Tap on the three dots in the upper right corner to open the image/video menu.

Tap Edit. This will take you to the page where you can edit the description of the file in question and tag people associated with it.

Enter relevant hashtags. To do this, enter the hash symbol (#) before each word.. Always make sure you use relevant tags; inappropriate use of hashtags is frowned upon.

Tap 'Done' or the checkmark ('✓'). You have finally added hashtags to your photo!

Add hashtags to a new photo

Tap the camera icon. It should be at the bottom of the screen, in the middle.

Click on it to take a photo or record a video. Select 'Library' and then the 'Photos' or 'Videos' option at the bottom of the screen.
If you want to publish an existing file, select it from your library. Then click Next and select a filter if you want to add one.

If you want to use a new image, use the round button to take the image. Select a filter and make the appropriate changes according to your preferences.

Add tags in the description. Always make sure they are relevant; for example, if it is a photo of a bakery, you could use words like "#muffin".
Adjust your hashtags. If you're trying to grow your Instagram account, avoid using hashtags that are too big, like #beauty or #fashion, because there are millions of posts in those categories; yours would get lost in seconds. Instead, create specific tags - even a personal tag that people can identify with. One way to find tags is to look at other successful profiles in your niche and use the same tags they do.
Tap OK to save the hashtags.

Tap Share. Your photo will now be visible to everyone, complete with hashtags!

To get the most out of hashtags, choose words that match for both your photo and your target audience.

If you overuse hashtags, especially if you use misleading ones to attract more users, will be considered spam.

CHAPTER 4

PUBLISH A VIDEO

You can record and upload videos directly in the Instagram app by tapping the camera icon on the home screen and holding down the record button. Before posting a video to your profile, you can use some editing options such as adding filters, changing the cover, and adding captions/hashtags. Videos can also be shared via your Stories, which are a collection of photos or videos that can be viewed by your followers in the Stories section but do not appear in your feed. These videos are automatically deleted after 24 hours. Remember that posted videos are public unless you send them via direct message or your profile is private.

Adding videos to your profile

Open the Instagram application. If you don't have it installed yet, you can download it from the Play Store or the App Store.

Sign in to your account. Tap "Sign in", enter your username and password, then tap "Sign in" again.

Tap the camera icon. This button is located in the center of the bottom menu bar and opens the camera.
The menu bar will not appear if you are in Settings or Direct Message area.

Select "Video". This button is located at the bottom right of the menu bar and activates video mode. When prompted, tap "Allow" to allow Instagram to access your camera.
At the bottom left, you can also select 'Gallery' to upload a video you've already saved on your device.

Tap and hold the 'Record' button, represented by a large circle at the bottom of the screen. Recording stops as soon as you remove your finger from the button.
You can record multiple clips and insert them into a video by pressing the button again after lifting your finger. Unwanted clips can be removed by tapping Delete under the record button (the last clip recorded will be deleted first).
Videos must be at least 3 seconds long and no longer than 60 seconds.
You can tap the round button at the bottom left of the recording screen to switch between the front and rear cameras.
You can activate the flash by tapping the flash icon at the bottom right of the recording area.

Tap "Next" to continue loading. This button is located in the upper right corner and opens the edit page.

Activate audio. Tap the speaker icon at the top of the screen to turn the sound on or off (if you see an "x" next to the icon, the sound is off). When you are satisfied with the final result, tap "Next".

Enlarge the video (iOS). iOS devices have a button next to the sound icon. Tapping this button will allow you to zoom in the video a bit. Tap "Next" when you are satisfied with the result.

Add a filter. If you have Android, tap "Filter" at the bottom left corner. If you have an iOS device, tap the icon with the overlapping circles (at the top of the screen). Scroll left or right in the list at the bottom of the screen to see the different color/lighting filters available. Tap "Next" when you have reached the desired effect.
Tap the Play button on the video screen to preview the selected filter.

Select the video cover. Tap "Cover" at the bottom right corner (Android) or the square icon at the top center of the screen (iOS). Tap an image in the video sequence to set it as a thumbnail for the video. This image will appear in your Instagram feed before the video plays. Tap "Next" when you are satisfied with the result.

Tap "Next" to continue uploading. A page with information about the video will open.

Add a description. Tap the caption field to enter a relevant comment or description. Tap "Share" when you're done.
In the video caption, you can tag friends or add hashtags by entering "@username" and "#hashtag".

Tap "Add location". You can select a location from a list of nearby locations or add a location tag to the video.

Link it to other social networks. You can select other social networks where you want to share the video by tapping the appropriate icon and entering your login details when prompted.

Make sure that "Follower" (Android) or "New Post" (iOS) is selected. The "Follower" tab appears in the upper left corner and the "New Post" button appears in the top center. Both are selected by default.
The alternative is "Direct Message", which allows you to share the video privately instead of posting it. You can select the users you want to send it to from your follower list and send it to them without posting it publicly.

Tap "Share". This button is located in the upper right corner and allows you to finish uploading the video to your Instagram profile.

Post a video via Instagram Stories

Open the Instagram app. If you don't have it installed yet, you can download it from the Play Store or App Store.

Sign in to your account. Tap "Sign in," enter your username and password, then tap "Sign in" again.

Tap the "Home" icon. This button is located at the bottom right and opens your Instagram feed.

Tap the "Your Story" icon. This button represents a "+" in a circle and is located in the upper left corner. Your device's camera will open.
You can also access this page by swiping to the right anywhere in your feed.

Tap and hold the 'Record' button. When you' re done, release to stop recording. The upload options will appear on the screen.
You can also scroll down to open a list of recent photos or videos.

Tap the speaker icon to activate the video sound. This button is located in the upper left corner. If it is flanked by an 'x', the sound has been disabled.

Tap "A" to enter text content into the video. Enter the text using the keyboard and it will appear on the screen. When you are done, tap "Finish" in the upper right corner or anywhere on the screen.

When you have finished entering text, you can tap and drag the text to move it to another location on the screen.

Tap the pen icon to draw on the screen. The drawing can be dragged anywhere on the screen. Tap the "Undo" button in the upper left corner to remove the last strokes and "Finish" to complete the process.

You can choose between different thicknesses/tip effects by tapping the icons at the top of the screen.

You can choose between different colors by tapping the buttons at the bottom of the screen.

Tap "Send to" to upload the video to your story. This button is located at the bottom right. The video can be viewed by your followers in the Story area or by tapping on your profile photo (but will not appear in your feed).

You can also tap the "Delete" button in the top left to cancel the upload, or "Download" in the top center of the screen to save it and upload the story later.

Photos and videos from stories disappear after 24 hours.

Tips

You can also upload videos directly from the Photos app (if you have the Instagram app installed) by opening a video, tapping the Share button, and selecting Instagram from the list of options.

Instagram collages cannot be used with videos.

You can mark your profile as private by tapping the human silhouette icon, opening the settings menu (which shows three dots vertically on Android and a cog on iOS), and activating the "Private Account" button. Posts for private accounts are only shared with followers. If a profile is public, all posts will be shared publicly.

CHAPTER 5

WHEN TO POST ON INSTAGRAM

What time zone should you consider when posting on Instagram?

When should I post on Instagram? Keep the time zone in mind! The more popular your brand is, the more time zones you need to consider when posting on Instagram. Some brands and influencers post the same post at different times depending on the time zone of their followers. Ideally, you want to make sure you reach as many time zones as possible without posting the same post multiple times. Avoid posting the same post more than four times a day, but try to post your content at different times to reach as many time zones as possible.

What countries are your customers from? If you are targeting residents of the United States and Canada, consider the EST time zone, as this is where most people live (including New York and Toronto). If your target audience is in London or the UK, then you will post according to GMT.

There are several social media analytics tools you can use to find out where your customers are coming from. Using this data, you can decide when to post on Instagram, figure out when to post on Instagram and other social media based on your followers and audience.

When should I post on Instagram?

The best time to post on Instagram is around lunchtime (11 am to 1 pm) and in the evening when most people have finished work (between 7 pm and 9 pm). Most Instagrammers visit the app from their mobile phones, so they are usually not online during working hours. Here are the posting times on Instagram:

The best days to post are Monday, Wednesday, and Thursday. Sunday is the worst day to post on Instagram, while the best time of the week is Saturday at 5 pm.
Wednesday is the day of the week with the most interactions on Instagram.
When to post on Instagram
What is the best time to post on Facebook?
As well as considering when to post on Instagram, you should also consider when to post on Facebook. To ensure that as many followers as possible see your posts, the best time to post on Facebook is during the week between 1 pm and 4 pm, during working hours. This is because many Facebook users surf from their computers, so they check their feed during

their free time of the day. However, the best time to post on Facebook is on Sundays at 3 pm.

The best days to post on Facebook are Thursday, Friday, Saturday, and Sunday. Tuesday is the worst day of the week to post on Facebook.
Weekends have the highest interaction on Facebook.
When to post on Facebook
When should you post on LinkedIn?
The best time to post on LinkedIn is between 10 and 11 am. LinkedIn is a professional social network used by job recruiters, salespeople, and business people, so it is most active during working hours.

Tuesday, Wednesday, and Thursday are usually the best days to post on LinkedIn.
The worst times to post on LinkedIn if you want to get interaction and visibility are weekends and out-of-business hours.
when to post on Linkedin
The best time to post on Twitter
The best time to post on Twitter is around lunchtime, between 12 and 1 p.m. However, scheduling posts just before lunchtime also works very well!

On weekdays, interaction on Twitter is very high. If you post from Monday to Friday during lunchtime, you can increase the interaction on your social profile.

Wednesday is the best day to post on Twitter. The weekend is the worst time to post on Twitter.
When you should post on Twitter
The best time to post on Pinterest
Now you know when to post photos on Instagram. What about Pinterest? The best time to post on Pinterest is in the evening, between 8 pm and 11 pm. It seems that moms are actively using Pinterest, which could be one of the reasons why the platform is more active in the late evening.

Saturday is currently the best day of the week to post on Pinterest, but Sunday is also a good day.
Working hours seem to be less popular among Pinterest users. Posting during these hours can lead to low interaction.
When to post on Pinterest
The best time to post videos on YouTube
Now that you know when to post your videos on Instagram, consider when to post them on YouTube. The best time to post to YouTube seems to be early afternoon, between 12 and 4 pm. Most users watch videos in the evening, so you need to post in the early afternoon so that your videos are indexed in the evening and easier to find.

Thursday and Friday are the best days to post on YouTube. Most people watch YouTube videos during the weekend. So you can also post videos on Saturday and Sunday, as long as you do it early in the morning, between 9 and 11 am.
When to post on youtube
When to post on Instagram and other social networks

When deciding when to post on Instagram and other social networks, you need to consider the type of platform you are using and the time zone of most of your customers.

The times we've given here are averages: If you analyze the interaction on your channels, you'll see that your followers are active at different times. The best way to find out when to post on social media is to experiment. You can use social management tools to schedule posts at different times in different weeks and see which days and times work best with your followers.

Also, don't forget to keep an eye on your competitors. Follow their progress and try to figure out when their posts have the highest interaction. The chances are very high that these times will work well with your followers. Test these times, and also try to post when they don't. Experiment. Also, remember that each platform is different, so analyze this data for each social platform to get the best results!

Google Analytics for social media analysis

Google Analytics provides all the information you need to decide when to post on Instagram and other social media. All you need to do is set up your social profiles and post a few updates to start collecting data. All you need to do is set up custom reports for each platform and start analyzing the information. Here's how:

Click Custom Reports in the left menu of Google Analytics.
Google Analytics report
Select "New custom report" to start creating your report.
Google Analytics custom report
Select the information you want to display in your report. Here you can see a basic Facebook report that shows you how to fill in the relevant fields, but you can track up to 10 metrics.
Facebook report for Google Analytics
Save the report and view the results. To display the time of day, just select "time of day" as a secondary dimension.
Google Analytics for Facebook
Repeat this process for all your main social channels.
Start by matching the times of your social media posts with this data.
Use custom reports to track your progress.
Social media management tools
Once you know when you should post on Instagram and other social channels, you can use social media management tools like Buffer, Later and Hootsuite to schedule your posts at any time. These tools help you to always post at the same time so you can interact with your followers even when you're asleep! They can also be used to determine which time zone has the highest level of interaction. Also, use these tools to publish the same post several times in different time zones to reach all your followers and redirect traffic to your website.

CHAPTER 6

GET A THOUSAND FOLLOWERS

Optimize your profile

Choose a theme for your profile. Themes serve two important purposes: they allow you to target and organize your photos, and they ensure that users always know the general style of the content they will see on your profile. Users can also get an idea of your personality.

Themes also help simplify content creation, as having boundaries to adhere to is often better than total freedom.

Add a relevant and informative biography. You should mention your subject, your website (if you have one), and something interesting about yourself or your artistic process. We all have a motivation that makes it interesting how or why we do something; find your element of originality and mention it in your bio!

You can also add tags to your bio if there are specific tags associated with your content.

Choose an attention-grabbing profile photo. If there is a photo that captures the essence of your topic, your content, and your personality, use it. If not, find an image that comes closest; people should be able to look at your profile picture and bio and have an idea of what to expect.

Link your Instagram profile to social media. You can link Instagram to Facebook, Twitter, Tumblr, and other platforms so you can post your Instagram information on all the sites you use. This way you gain followers from people who already follow you on other social networks and get more exposure.

Never make your Instagram posts private. If you're trying to grow your follower base, one of the downsides is that you can't protect your profile from people you don't know, otherwise you'll alienate potential followers. Make sure your account is public, easy to follow and you'll see the followers coming.

Involve other users

Follow people who share your interests. It's not a mistake to follow as many people as possible in the hope that they will return the favor, but focus on accounts that post content that inspires you. These profiles are more likely to follow you, so you maximize your time compared to following random users.

Like people's photos. For every 100 likes, you'll get about 8 followers, assuming you choose photos from average accounts rather than celebrities.
Although you probably won't reach 1000 followers with this method alone, it's a good start.

Leave meaningful comments on photos. It is well known that commenting on other users' photos leads to an increase in followers. Unfortunately, this means that many people write one- or two-word comments in the hope of being followed. If you leave a well-constructed comment, the chances increase that the creator will decide to become your follower.
For example, on a photo of a DIY personal office, you might write: "Wow, I love your new office! I'd love to see a tutorial on how you built it!" instead of "Cute" or "Looks good".

Write comments to users with few followers. In some cases, it's best to leave a cute comment for people who post content you like. By doing so, you not only make them happy but also encourage them to follow you, especially if you are already a follower.
Remember that sending a message to someone can be interpreted as an invasion of their privacy. Write politely and respectfully when contacting another user.
Never ask another user to follow you.

Post regularly. You could post just once a week and it wouldn't be a problem! However, try to always follow the same pattern (or even increase the frequency from time to time) to meet your followers' expectations. You will lose followers if your content arrives too late.

This advice is more likely to maintain your current following than grow it.

Try not to post more than a few times a day.

Post at the right time of day. Mornings (7 am-9 pm), early afternoons (11 am-2 pm), and late afternoons (5 pm-7 pm) are the busiest times of day on Instagram, so try to make the most of them by posting at these times.

These times are based on Italian time zones, so adjust accordingly if you're abroad.

If you can't stick to these times, don't worry; several studies have shown that posting at these times is useful, but not essential.

Photo tags

Use tags in all your photos. The easiest way to do this is to write a description, leave a few spaces underneath (usually using dots to separate them), and then include any relevant tags.

Experiment with the most popular tags. Sites like https://top-hashtags.com/instagram/ have a list of the 100 most used hashtags of the day, so try including some of them in your post descriptions.

Remember that some tags are so overused that they make it difficult to find your post.

Don't just use popular tags.

Create your hashtag. If you want, you can create your hashtag or use one that is not often used. Try to include it in all your posts as if it were a signature for your profile.

Use a geotag for your photos. Use geotags to add the geographic location where the photo was taken to the post so that anyone nearby can find it.

Don't use irrelevant tags. Do not include tags in the description of the photo that does not represent it in any way, as this practice is often considered spam.

The path to 1000 followers should be taken step by step. Don't rush, follow these strategies and you will reach your goal.

The more proactive you are on Instagram, the sooner you will build your user base.

Post as often as possible, but don't resort to spam. Don't post content every hour or every minute; it's just annoying and users may decide not to follow you.

Like other users' posts, especially those with few followers.

Never mistreat people on Instagram or any other social platform; people will see your true colors and stop following you and talking to you.

Never post a person's photo without their consent.

Don't post many photos at the same time or the same photo more than once.

CHAPTER 7

FIND OUT WHO IS NO LONGER FOLLOWING YOU ON INSTAGRAM

Using the Instagram app

Launch the Instagram app. Tap on the corresponding icon, which shows a multicolored stylized labeled camera. If you are already signed in, you will see the main page of your account.

If you're not yet signed in to Instagram, tap the Sign in link and enter your email address (or username or phone number) and security password.

Tap the profile icon labeled AndroidIGprofile.png. It is located in the bottom right corner of the screen.

Select the follower option. It will be displayed at the top of the screen along with the total number of followers you have. For example, if you currently have 100 people following you, tap on the 100 followers icon.

Scroll down the list of followers to see which ones are missing. Scroll through your follower list to find the names of people who are no longer present. If a particular user you knew was a follower is no longer on your list, they have stopped following you.

This is difficult if you have a large number of followers, but you should still be able to get an idea of who is no longer following you if you have had the opportunity to interact with them or if you are a follower.

It is possible that the user in question who is no longer following you may have closed their account. In this case, use the search function (indicated by a small magnifying glass) to check if their Instagram account is still active by searching for the username.

Using the Instagram website

Go to the Instagram website. Enter the URL https://www.instagram.com/ into the address bar of your computer's internet browser. If you are already logged in with your account, you will be redirected to your home page.

If you are not yet logged in, click on the Log In link at the bottom of the page and then enter your username (or email address or phone number) and security password.

Click on the "Profile" icon image titled AndroidIGprofile.png. It shows a stylized human silhouette in the upper right corner of the page.

Click on the "Followers" item. It is located at the top of the page along with your total number of followers.
For example, if you currently have 100 people following you, click the 100 followers icon.

Check the list of followers to see which ones are missing. If a particular user you knew was a follower is no longer on your list, they have stopped following you.
This is difficult if you have a large number of followers, but you should still be able to get an idea of who has stopped following you if you have interacted with them or if you are a follower yourself.
Keep in mind that the user in question who has stopped following you may have closed their account. In this case, use the search bar at the top of the page to see if their Instagram account is still active by searching for the username.

Using the Follow Cop app on Android

Understand how the app works. Follow Cop is an app (created exclusively for Android platforms) that allows you to keep track of Instagram followers who are no longer following you. Unfortunately, Follow Cop requires you to enter your Instagram account login details to view your follower list and see who has unfollowed you.
Follow Cop is not able to track the full history of all the followers you've lost in the past, as it only tracks changes from the date of installation.

Instagram Marketing Blueprint 2023

Although the Follow Cop app does not create or edit posts on your Instagram profile, once installed you will automatically become a follower of the app's social network page.

If you want to use this method on a computer, you will need to download and install the BlueStacks Android emulator to install the app on your system.

Download the Follow Cop app. Access the Google Play Store by tapping on the image icon titled Androidgoogleplay.png and then follow these instructions:

Select the search bar.

Enter the keywords, follow cop.

Tap on the Unfollowers for an Instagram app, Follow Cop.

Press the Install button.

Press the Accept button when prompted;

If you chose to access the Google Play Store using the Bluestacks emulator, click on the My Apps tab in the top left corner of the app window, click on the System Apps folder, and click on the Play Store icon.

Launch the Follow Cop application. Press the Open button located on the Google Play Store page. Alternatively, tap the Follow Cop app icon on the home screen of your device. This will take you to the app's login page.

Sign in to your Instagram account. Enter your profile username and security password in the "Username" and "Password" text boxes, then press the "Sign In" button.

Select your account. Tap on your Instagram profile, visible at the top of the screen.

Select the Recently unfollowed option. It's in the middle of the page.

Close the advertising banner that appears, if necessary. Tap on the X or Close icon visible in one of the corners of the screen. You will automatically return to the Recent Unfollowed screen so that the Follow Cop app can start tracking your followers.
Some banners require you to wait between 5 and 10 seconds before you can close them by tapping the X icon.

Close Follow Cop and reopen it when you want to check the status of your followers. If you go back to the Current Unfollowers screen in the app, you can see a full list of the names of everyone who has unfollowed you since you installed the app.
You may see several banner ads before you can access the Recent Unfollowers tab in the Follow Cop app.

In some cases, it's best to compare the number of people currently following you with the result of a previous count. For example, if you had 120 followers yesterday and only 100 today, you've lost 20 followers. Of course, this is a quantitative check and not a qualitative one, as you don't know who is no longer following you, but if you are only interested in statistics, it doesn't matter which people are no longer following you compared to the total number of followers you have lost.

Since Instagram has prevented most third-party web services and apps from interacting with its platform, tools such as the Follow Cop app will likely be short-lived.

CHAPTER 8

INSTAGRAM CONTACT

Create a report from your computer

Go to the Instagram Help Centre website. Visit the URL https://help.instagram.com/ using your favorite browser. Unfortunately, there is no way to contact Instagram's customer service or support staff directly. There's no phone number you can call, no text message you can send, and no email address you can write to get in touch directly with a live operator who can answer your questions. You can only try to resolve your issue using the Instagram Help Centre website.

Click on the Privacy and Security tab. It is displayed on the left side of the main page.

Click on the Content Report link. It's located at the bottom of the left side of the page, where all the options are displayed.

Select the category that the problem you want to report falls into. A list of options is displayed on the left side of the page, so select the one that best suits your needs.
Accounts that have been hacked: Select this if you believe your account has been hacked.

Accounts impersonating other people or companies: Select this if you're sure an Instagram account is impersonating you.

Children under 13: Click this option if you think you've spotted an account run by a teenager under the age of 13.

Accounts promoting hateful content: Click this option if you want to report violent content, intimidation, or bullying.

Dissemination of private information: Select this option if you have identified an account where personal or sensitive information about a user (such as their home address or mobile phone number) has been published.

Self-harm: Click this option to report posts where a user clearly states that they intend to inflict physical harm on themselves.

Offensive actions and spam: Click this option to report misconduct, inappropriate content, spam, or harassment.

Exploitation: Select this option to learn more about reporting issues related to child exploitation, human trafficking, or animal trafficking.

Other types of reports: Click this option if you don't see the category or topic that the reason for your Instagram report falls under in the list displayed.

Answer any questions you have. Depending on the category you chose for your report, you may have to answer some questions, select additional options from the drop-down menus, and fill out a form. In the latter case, always try to describe the problem clearly. Always provide as many details as possible, as long as they are relevant to solving the problem. Explain clearly why and how the reported content violates Instagram's rules. Follow these instructions depending on the problem you are reporting.

Hacked accounts: Select one of the links in the Hacked Accounts section and follow the instructions.

Accounts impersonating other people or organizations: Select one of the links in the "Accounts impersonating other people or organizations" section and follow the instructions.

Children under 13: Click on the How to report the presence of... link, click on the blue part of the text "Fill out this form", enter the account information to be reported and click the Submit button.

Accounts spreading hateful content: Click on the link "Report intimidating or bullying content on Instagram", click on the blue part of the text "Send a report", fill in the form displayed with the required information, and click on the Submit button.

Sharing private information: Click on the blue part of the text "Report us", fill in the form that appears with the required information, and then click the "Submit" button.

Self-harming: Select one of the links displayed in the "Self-harming" box according to the issue you wish to report, click on the appropriate option, if any, to report it, fill out the form with the required information and then click the Submit button.

Offensive acts and spam: Select one of the links displayed in the Offensive acts and spam box, click on the appropriate option, if any, to report it, fill out the form with the required information and then click the Submit button.

Exploitation: Select one of the links displayed in the Exploitation box for detailed instructions on how to make a report of child exploitation, wildlife exploitation, or human trafficking.

Other types of reports: Select one of the links displayed in the main field of the page, click on the blue text part of the action you want to take (e.g. "Send us a report", "Contact us", "Fill in this form" or "Let us know"), fill in a form that appears on the screen with the required information and then click on the Submit button.

Wait for the problem to be resolved. Likely, you will not receive a response from Instagram staff, but rest assured that your report will be taken into account. If the problem you reported is not resolved within one working week, you can make a second report. Alternatively, you can visit the Instagram Helpdesk website and select which category of an issue the problem you are reporting falls into from the list of available options on the left. If you need help with your account or using the mobile app, Instagram's support center is the best resource you have for resolving the issue.

Create a report from a mobile device

Launch the Instagram app. A multicolored camera icon will appear. If you have already logged in with your account, you will be taken to the main profile page.

If you haven't signed in yet, you'll need to enter the email address and password of the Instagram account you want to use.

Tap on the icon or image of your profile photo titled AndroidIGprofile.png. It will appear in the bottom right corner of the screen. Your Instagram profile page will be displayed.

Unfortunately, there is no way to contact Instagram's customer service or support staff directly. There is no phone number to call, no text message to send, and no email address to write to in order to get in touch directly with a live operator who can listen to your questions. The only way to try and solve your problem is to use the Instagram helpdesk website.

Press the gear-shaped button (on iPhone) or the ⋮ icon (on Android). Both will appear in the top right corner of the screen. The main menu of the Instagram app will appear.

Scroll down and select the "Report a problem" option. This will appear in the 'Support' section at the bottom of the screen displayed.

Select one of the available options. You can choose from the following problem categories.

Report spam or abuse (on iPhone) or Report spam or abuse (on Android): you will be redirected to the Instagram support page.

Something isn't working o Report a problem: You'll see a text box where you can enter a description of the problem.
General comments o Post a comment: You will see a text box where you can enter a comment.

Follow the guidelines that correspond to the option you have chosen. Depending on the type of report you want to create and which you selected in the previous step, you will receive different instructions.

Report spam or abuse (on iPhone) or report spam or abuse (on Android): Use the resources in the Instagram Help Centre.

Something isn't working or Report a problem: Enter a description of the problem you want to report, then press the Submit or ✓ button. If you are using an Android device, you can attach a screenshot of the problem to your report by pressing the + button.

General comments or writes a comment: Enter your comment and press the Submit or ✓ button. If you are using an Android device, you can attach a screenshot to the report by pressing the + button.

Wait for the problem to be resolved. Likely, you won't receive any feedback from Instagram staff, but they will try to fix the issue you reported within a week of receiving your message. In the meantime, visit the Instagram Helpdesk site and look at the list of options available to you on the left side of the page, so you can choose which category the issue you want to report falls into. If you need help with your account or using the mobile app, Instagram's support center is the best resource you have for resolving the issue.

Report a post

Launch the Instagram app. A multicolored camera icon will appear. If you are already signed in with your account, you will be taken to the main profile page.
If you are not yet signed in, you will need to enter the email address and password of the Instagram account you want to use.

Find the post you want to report. It can appear directly in your home once you've logged into the Instagram app. Alternatively, select the magnifying glass icon at the bottom of the screen and type the name of the account that published the post in question into the search bar that appears at the top of the page. Then tap on the profile name and search for the offending post directly on the Instagram page of the user who published it.

Press the : button that appears in the Post to Report box. It has three vertically aligned dots and is located in the top right corner of each post. A context menu will appear.

Select the Report option. This is one of the items listed in the menu that appears after pressing the button with the three dots.

Select either It's spam or It's not appropriate. If the post contains illegal, pornographic, or violent material, select Not appropriate. If the post has already been published several times or has been created for commercial purposes (e.g. to try to sell a product or service), select the Spam option. The corresponding post will be reported immediately.

It is not possible to report ads published directly by Instagram as spam. However, if you feel that the content of a particular ad is inappropriate, you can tap on the three-dot icon and select the Report adoption.

Troubleshooting

Block a persistent or harassing user. If someone is constantly harassing you on Instagram, the quickest and easiest way to solve the problem is to block that person's account.

If the user in question is threatening or harassing you, you can make a report via the Instagram Help Centre website.

Change your Instagram password often. To prevent your account from being hacked or compromised by an attacker, try to change your security password at least once every six months.

If you need to reset your Instagram password without knowing your current password, follow these instructions.

Consider making your account private. If you change your account from public to private, people who don't currently

follow you won't be able to see your posts and content on Instagram until you accept their request to become your follower. To make an account private via the mobile app, follow these instructions:
- Launch the Instagram app;
- Tap the image of your profile icon titled AndroidIGprofile.png;
- Press the gear-shaped button (on iPhone) or the button marked with three dots ⋮ (on Android);
- Activate the "Private Account" slider by sliding it to the right;
- Press the Yes button when prompted.

Temporarily deactivate your Instagram account. If you're dealing with comments or complaints from a group of users or followers who are a little too pushy or energetic, or if you feel like you need to get some energy back, deactivating your account for a while maybe, the best solution. You can reactivate it at any time by simply logging in.

Warnings

Instagram does not have a phone number to contact a customer service representative. So if you visit a website or webpage that lists a Facebook or Instagram customer service phone number, it's a scam.

CHAPTER 9

INSTAGRAM STORIES

Since 2016, there has been a new feature on Instagram for Business that allows businesses and users to produce different content (both photos and videos) throughout the day and combine them into a slideshow: Instagram Stories.

Today, stories are everywhere!

The main innovation is that companies don't have to worry about the risk of posting too much content, as the photos and videos included in Stories disappear after 24 hours and don't appear in the news feed of the company profile.

However, if you particularly like a piece of content in your story, you can post it on your profile.

In addition, businesses can get creative with Instagram Stories by using editing tools that allow you to write and draw your newly created content.

Users can see the Stories posted by the profiles they follow via a horizontal bar at the top of their feed and easily identify new content that is posted thanks to a colored ring that appears around it.

Viewing Stories is very simple: a simple swipe left or right is all it takes to switch profiles, and a blue bar at the top shows users viewing a Story how much content it consists of, so those viewing photos and videos posted within a Story can make sure they don't skip any content before switching sides. There are also no public likes or comments. If a user wants to comment on a content posted in a story, they can contact the person who posted it directly through Instagram Direct or by using emoticons.

Instagram Stories follows the privacy settings of your account. If you have a private account, your Stories will only be visible to your followers.

However, you can also hide the entire story from very specific profiles that you don't want to see the content, even if they follow you. Want to know who has seen your story? Swipe up while viewing your story and see who has viewed each piece of content in it.

Adding to this is another first for Instagram: Instead of just focusing on getting more views, maybe it's time to turn to Instagram Stories stickers as well.

Stickers offer a free, easy and fun way to interact with your followers and get them excited about your brands, content, and products.

Questions, polls, GIFs, and new stickers, such as the 'countdown' or the feature to add music to your Instagram Stories, have proven to be a creative and personal way to encourage people to interact with you. You can also create stickers that match your branding to use not only on your own stories but also on those of your fans.

The good news is that it's super quick and easy to create GIFs for Instagram - you can simply open a Giphy channel and create GIFs that relate to your business.

There's one thing that every business on Instagram has in common: a desire for more engagement.

Instagram's algorithm prioritizing personal content has meant that posts on Instagram feeds aren't seen as often as they used to be. If you're getting fewer impressions on your posts, you're also likely to see a drop in engagement.

Engagement on Instagram feed posts has been steadily declining for a few years now. It's time to change your definition of "engagement" and focus on engaging your followers through Instagram Stories instead of your regular posts.

Instagram Stories have exploded in popularity in the last two years, with over 400 million people viewing them every day. Instagram Stories is the most exciting marketing innovation on the entire social platform, thanks to it Instagram is increasingly becoming the social media platform of the 'now', more immediate than ever, with ephemeral content that creates urgency.

Treat Stories as a social channel in its own right, monitor traffic from Stories separately from traffic generated by the bio link on Instagram.

Just as you have an editorial plan with a content calendar for your Instagram, Twitter, and Facebook channels, you need to do the same for Instagram Stories in 2022.

Try Instagram Stories ad campaigns while they are still relatively new and cheap because this ad platform will explode in 2023.

Instagram Stories VS Snapchat

Now that you know all the features of Instagram Stories, is there anything that sounds familiar?

Many have noticed many (too many) similarities with Snapchat and many have wondered if Facebook has openly copied Evan Spiegel's platform.

A half-hearted admission came from Instagram CEO Kevin Systrom, who admitted in an interview with TechCrunch that he has to give all the credit to Snapchat.

Instagram Stories aims to increase user engagement by making content more ephemeral and engaging. Today, we can say that Instagram Stories has become an indispensable tool in your marketing activities on Instagram.

The fact that this content is no longer available after 24 hours means that people are always waiting for new videos or images that the company publishes. Of course, to achieve this effect, you need to develop a real story with a plotline that engages the user.

No one would pay to watch a movie where there is a sequence of disjointed photos and videos that don't follow a coherent path.

Even though Instagram and Snapchat are free, the concept is the same. Would you spend your time seeing content that is not relevant and doesn't follow a clear path?

When using Instagram Stories, businesses need to be able to create an engaging story that captures the user and keeps them waiting for the next piece of content.

Both Snapchat and Instagram Stories appeal to a different audience than those found on other social networks such as Facebook.

It is now clear that Snapchat targets a niche audience, just like Twitter.

Firstly, both appeal to younger users who are more creative and tend to create content.

Secondly, they appeal to users who are willing to experiment. In this regard, we can say that one of the biggest advantages of Instagram Stories is that it simplifies Snapchat's posting dynamic and also makes it more understandable for a more traditionalist audience who are used to communicating in a certain way and find it difficult to get into Snapchat's dynamic.

Unfortunately, we don't know who will win the long battle for innovation between Zuckerberg and Spiegel, but what we do know is that businesses can only benefit.

PART II – INSTAGRAM BUSINESS

CHAPTER 10

MAKING MONEY WITH INSTAGRAM

Instagram is one of the fastest-growing marketing tools of this generation. So, with a little patience and some technical knowledge, anyone can make a money. By creating a curated account with quality content, attracting brands or photo sites, and generating content that people are willing to pay for, you too can make money on Instagram!

Create an interesting account

Choose a creative but accurate username. Once your account becomes popular, people will talk about it using the exact username you chose. Therefore, it should be memorable, original, and easy to pronounce.
The name should reflect the theme. For example, if you are an artist, you should use a username inspired by your real name (or a pseudonym).

Enrich the description in a relevant way. You can provide different information to other users.

Describe your content and/or objective accurately but concisely.

If you have one, provide a link to your website.

Enter the email address you use for work. You may want to create a separate account for your Instagram account.

Enter the username you have on other social networks (such as Twitter or Facebook).

Enter the name you've chosen for any instant messaging services you use.

Enter your PayPal or Venmo email address to receive donations.

Share your CV. Post it on a static blog page first and then link to it in your description - this is the best way to share your CV.

Choose a topic to cover. Unlike your personal Instagram or Facebook profile, everything you post on your new account should have a unique theme (like fitness or food).

In short, find something that you think is needed (or something that the company could benefit from) and that allows you to express your talents.

Make sure your content complies with Instagram's terms of use.

Refine your posts and post descriptions. Among other things, make sure your photos look good using filters and other editing tools and include relevant information in the description.

For example, if you are promoting, include in the photo description a short sentence about the product or service you are promoting, explain how it improves life, and add relevant links.

Posts are usually most successful between 2 am and 5 pm. Make sure you publish them at these times, taking into account the specific time zone of your target market.

As you grow, stay true to what you stand for. Above all, don't focus on monetization. Your job is to create content and that should be your priority. Don't betray the followers who love your content: Think about what your audience wants to see and offer it to them. Your followers are your most important parameter and you should never sacrifice them.

Post several times a day. Although it is important not to overwhelm followers with content, it is a good idea to offer quality posts several times a day.

Try to vary your content while staying on the main topic: you shouldn't stray too far from your usual posts, but you shouldn't post the same thing every day either.

Read the comments under posts. Users usually give feedback (explicit or implicit) that can help you tailor future posts to more followers.

It's impossible to take advantage of all the suggestions you receive, but try to focus on the most common tips from your followers.

Maintain an active presence on Instagram to promote your account and increase the appreciation you generally receive:
Reply to comments often. Once you reach a certain number of followers, you won't be able to do this with everyone, but try to reply to a few users in every post.
Indicate that you like the posts of brands, users or accounts that you would like to collaborate with. This helps you to be altruistic while promoting your account.

Link your Instagram account to those of other social networks. These links should already be in the description, but it is important to update other social network pages with relevant content.
Facebook. Create and maintain a Facebook page dedicated to your topic on Instagram. You can then promote it on your profile.
Twitter. Create an account dedicated to the content covered on your Instagram profile. You can publish the same posts on Instagram and Twitter, but try to produce unique content for this social network as well.
The use of other sites depends on your target audience. For example, you can use Tumblr, YouTube, and Pinterest.

Attract and retain followers

Set yourself a target. The number of followers you should aim for depends on the topic of your profile. If you are applying to work with brands and run advertising campaigns, most companies require you to have around 10,000 followers before offering you a contract.

How many followers does it take to be considered an influencer?

On Instagram, you are usually considered a micro-influencer if you have more than 10,000 followers; a macro-influencer is when you have more than a million. But there are also several levels in between. Up to 100,000 followers, you usually get some free products and some modeling work from time to time if you fall into that bracket. However, the real monetization starts through partnerships that occur above 100,000 followers.

Use relevant hashtags in posts. If you want to target a specific audience (which is highly recommended), use hashtags that those users might search for. For example, if you have several photos of landscapes in northern Italy, you could tag the photos with "#northitaly" and "#landscapesnorthitaly".

Only use relevant hashtags for your post, as using clickbait or unreliable keywords will set potential followers back - not to mention have your account flagged as spam.

Declare that you like and comment on other accounts' photos. This will give you visibility: When other users see your likes and read your words, it will be easier for them to view your profile. For best results, use this tactic on users you want to be followed by.

You can do this on many random accounts to gain followers. This process takes a lot of time, but it is effective in gaining a following.

Promote your account on social networks. Profiles on other social networks should already be heavily highlighted in the description, but make sure your Instagram account is promoted just as heavily on other profiles.
Simply post a link to your Instagram account on your Facebook or Twitter profile to promote your content.

Facilitate engagement. To engage with your followers, it's a good idea to ask them to leave feedback or take certain actions. If your requests are interesting enough, you will attract more people. You can encourage the participation of other users in different ways.
Organise competitions with certain products or services as prizes. Invite other users to like and/or share the post to participate.
Ask questions. Encourage other users to respond, thus stimulating interest in the content you offer.
Accept requests. This directly involves users in creating future content, especially if you use Instagram as a photo showcase.

Use promotions. Try running a competition to get customers' attention. To participate, users must follow you on your Instagram profile. To make a post go viral, you can also invite them to tag their friends. If you're running a contest, make sure you follow the rules set by Instagram.

Listen to your followers. If you find that a particular complaint or request is quite common, don't ignore it. Instead, try to justify the feedback to satisfy followers in general. Remember that they are the ones who support you and help you grow!

Using affiliate marketing

Make sure you meet the requirements for marketing initiatives. You should be interested in promoting brands, have at least 500 followers, and can update/publish content regularly.
Affiliate marketing often requires you to take photos of yourself or others while showing or using a particular product or service.

Follow the brands you target. If you want your account to be noticed by a company, you need to be active on their pages. This will also help you better understand the features of their marketing strategy, such as their preferred tone, content style, and products/services.

Like and comment on your favorite brands' posts. If you do this often enough, you'll get their attention. You will be able to show that your account has great potential for its business goals.

Don't spam them with unnecessary comments or questions. Instead, post interesting ideas, feedback, or questions that have the potential to enrich their marketing tactics.

Look for a service that specializes in affiliate marketing. Several websites will help you work with businesses. Remember that you must first attract the attention of the brand you want to promote.

Shareasale: Create an account and then sign up to work for a specific brand. You earn a commission every time you get a user to contact a specific company through a link on your Instagram profile.

Stylinity: designed for the fashion world. When users buy from a website through your link, you earn a commission.

Reach out to businesses on social media. This shows that your account is well maintained. You can also contact marketing departments directly by e-mail.

This is one of the reasons why you should include the company email in the description. Once companies are ready to contact you, they can do so directly through your profile on Instagram.

Try to be patient. If your account is active and growing steadily, sooner or later companies will want to work with you, even if it's just for a little promotion in exchange for free products. You'll have to work your way up, so any marketing experience you can get - even for free - will help you add to your CV and get more interesting opportunities later on.

Sell photos

Try to sell your photos. This isn't for every Instagram account, but anyone with a smartphone that takes HD photos can try creating editing, and uploading photos. Sooner or later you will upload a photo that someone will be interested in.

Look for an app that helps you sell your photos. When other users see and buy your photos, their interest increases and you can use this for commercial purposes.
Foap is a useful app available for iPhone and Android. First, create an account and then upload your photos to the database. Users can view and buy your photos and you earn 50% of the total price.

Distinguish between stock and premium content. Stock content (i.e. low-quality photos that companies and websites can use for promotional purposes) should be published directly on your chosen photo selling app, while you should sell premium shots (i.e. very high-quality images that have a higher price tag) individually through your Instagram profile. At this point, it becomes important to have a good following. Remember that stock content should not be low quality: It should be more generic or otherwise adaptable to a variety of contexts. Premium content should be tailored to a specific use.

Sign premium photos. You can do this by uploading a low-resolution version of the image or adding a watermark (e.g. your signature or a distinctive phrase) over the photo. Avoid distributing original copies.
If a user wants to buy the photo, you can send them the version without a watermark and an invoice to receive payment.

Post signed photos with a price tag. Include the following information in the post:
- Desired price.
- Preferred payment method (e.g. PayPal or Venmo).
- Photo size.
- Resolution of the photo.
- Short description of the photo.

Wait for followers to request a photo. If you have an active following and have generated interest in your photos, you should have no problem selling some on Instagram!
You can also accept photo requests from individual followers and charge a premium price for these images.

Most marketing applications and businesses require a PayPal account to make payments.
If the theme of your profile is photography, make sure the photos you post are of high quality. One unintentionally

blurred or badly edited shot is enough to damage your credibility as a photographer.

In rare cases, it is possible to sell your Instagram account to make easy money.

If you are active, regularly post quality content and listen to your followers, you are likely to succeed on Instagram.

As with any business venture, building a reputation and monetizing takes time.

In several countries, advertising on Instagram must be declared by law by adding a hashtag such as "#ad" in the post description

CHAPTER 11

INSTAGRAM AND BRANDS

According to Iconosquare, in 2015, 62% of Instagram users were already following a brand on this platform. In contrast, a study found that Instagram offers businesses 58 times more opportunities for success than Facebook and 120 times more than Twitter.

This study looked at the seven largest social networks, of which six companies were able to achieve a user engagement rate of less than 0.1%. For Instagram, this figure reaches 4.21%.

The incredible level of interaction that can be achieved is due to the loyal and active nature of Instagram users.

Instagram can offer you more than you think

Building your brand or informing your customers is central to the operations of any successful business.

The fact that you landed on this content is already a great indicator that you are smart enough to understand and take seriously that Instagram is on the rise and the opportunities behind this social network are huge.

Don't ask why, but how to market (quickly) with Instagram
Instagram's rapid rise continues, eclipsing the stagnant growth rates of Snapchat and Facebook. This large audience is now a strong draw for IGTV, Instagram's newly launched video hub. While IGTV's monetization opportunities are already foreseeable in the future, content creators could gain new visibility and build their fan base even more.

It's proven that social networks are increasingly influencing users' purchasing decisions.

By finding the right mix of (relevant) content, you can generate more interest in your brand and push your users without having to invest too much in presentations and expensive push activities.

Why is Instagram a unique social network?
- It is completely mobile
- It is based on visual design
- It is virtually link-free
- The elements of success

To be successful on Instagram, it's not enough to just randomly post pretty pictures and images. Instead, you need to:
- Have a clear idea of your goals and strategy
- Post with a constant frequency
- Know your followers
- Have a clear style guide

By combining all these ingredients, you can reach your audience in a direct and targeted way, increase their interest, raise brand awareness and see an impressive return on investment.

The first important step in an Instagram marketing strategy is to define the goals you want to achieve.
Decide why you are on Instagram and set goals.
Even if you've never used this platform before or if you're just starting and results are still lacking, it's important to have clear goals in mind.

This way, the content you produce can be geared towards achieving these goals and be more consistent in the eyes of your followers.
Companies typically use Instagram to showcase their product or service, build a community, increase brand awareness, tell the company's story and values, increase brand loyalty, and share news and updates.

It is very important to decide on one or two goals. To do this, it can be helpful to answer these questions:
- Why use Instagram?
- How can Instagram help me achieve my marketing goals?
- How much time and budget should I invest in Instagram?
- What is different about Instagram compared to other social networks?

Your goals are to help you not only target the right audience but also create good and relevant content. This is very important because it influences everything you do on Instagram.

Choose 1-2 goals from this:
- Promote products or services (including selling on Instagram).
- Build new relationships
- Looking behind the scenes of the company
- Introducing the company's employees
- Representing the more informal and fun side of the business

The creative possibilities and visual aspects of Instagram, when strategically using Stories to showcase the personality and faces behind your brand, can be particularly powerful for highly visual businesses and a great way to creatively engage with customers and employees, reach out to your prospects, and build relationships with them.

Once you've defined your goals and metrics for assessing achievable results, it becomes important to understand which audience you want to target.

The main goal of marketing is to communicate the right message to your audience, at the exact moment they want it. Knowing the demographics of a platform's users is key to understanding whether you are reaching your target audience. We, therefore, recommend that you start by defining your buyer persona at the beginning.

Once you've defined your goals and determined the effectiveness of Instagram for your target audience, you can move on to the core of your strategy:

Is your company targeting a B2B audience? We recommend checking out Instagram B2B Marketing with this content.

How to optimize your Instagram profile

When someone searches for a keyword on Instagram, such as "lighting design", the accounts that have the keyword in their profile name are displayed.
The order or ranking of these accounts depends on how Instagram determines that they may be of interest to you.
If someone you follow follows an account associated with the keyword you entered, Instagram will display that account and include that information in the list. This immediately gives the user a reason to pick you out of all the others and builds more trust.
Think of your Instagram profile as a homepage.
In your profile, you have the opportunity to share some information about your business and include links to send visitors to your website. How can you optimize your Instagram profile?

By making the most of the following four elements, you can create great value for your users:
The company bio/description.

The description should be closely related to the brand. What you share in the short space that Instagram provides should be representative of your story, your offering, and your values, and should be able to explain to users what you're about. In addition, companies tend to include a tagline or slogan, such as Nike's 'Just Do It'. Larger companies may also include their hashtag in the description.

Profile photo

Your brand must be instantly recognizable when a user views your posts or visits your profile. For most businesses, this means using their logo, a brand name (the logo minus a few words), or a mascot as their profile picture.

Link

Unlike other social networks, Instagram does not allow you to add links to posts. The only area where you can add links is in your profile information. Many businesses tend to use this link to point to their homepage, but you can also use this option to direct visitors to a landing page or specific content. Only verified Instagram account holders can add links to their Instagram Stories, provided they have reached 10,000 followers or more.

Instagram business profile

In July, Instagram broke the news of the launch of a very useful new tool for all businesses: the Business profile. Currently, this feature is still in the testing phase and is only available in the US, New Zealand, and Australia, but will be available in other countries in the coming months. With this new tool, businesses can link their Instagram profile to their Facebook page, get insights and statistics on followers and posts, and promote targeted posts directly from the app. This allows you to see which posts are most successful, on which days and at what time of day your target group is most active, and who your audience is on Instagram. And that's not all. With this new feature, users can get in touch with the company directly from the app with a simple tap of the "Contact" button.

How to optimize your Instagram feed

If you want to succeed on Instagram, you can't overlook any element, so you need to pay attention to how your profile looks as a whole.

Your feed is the first opportunity you have to make a good impression and entice people to hit the "follow" button. And as your Instagram profile becomes as important as your homepage, you need to make sure it's up to date.

When someone visits your Instagram profile, they will decide within seconds whether or not to follow you by quickly scrolling through your feed, reading your bio, or clicking on highlights in your Stories.

When it comes to converting visitors into followers, it's no longer just the style of photo editing that needs to be consistent.

Fortunately, it's easy to create a professional-looking feed with a well-maintained and consistent Instagram aesthetic.

The stunning Instagram aesthetic is not a new trend on Instagram. Businesses of all sizes, from startups to super brands, have been curating their feeds to attract new followers for some time now.

Your feed doesn't have to adhere to the all-white, perfect Instagram aesthetic to be successful, it just needs to match your brand and your target market.

In 2023, it's important to make sure that every aspect of your feed and every post is consistent with the aesthetic you've chosen for your brand.

So whether you're posting to Instagram Stories, posting an IGTV video, or creating highlights for your profile page, you need to make sure everything aligns and represents your overall brand and Instagram aesthetic.

You can plan the look of your feed and Instagram aesthetic using a third-party Instagram marketing platform. There are many available today.

Use a good program or photo editing app.

When it comes to editing and enhancing your photos, you need a reliable photo editing program with features that can reduce editing time.

It's a good investment, not only to make your Instagram feed look good but also to get more Instagram followers.

Creating a cohesive Instagram feed can be achieved by using the same 1-2 filters or presets for each photo.

This makes it much easier to put all your photos together and also reduces editing time.

How to create an effective content marketing strategy on Instagram

Identify the pillars of your content
Photo and video content is the heart of Instagram.
The more than 100 million photos and videos shared on the platform every day are proof of this.

But what should the content you add be about?

Before thinking about visual content, style, and design, it is useful to have an overview of the message you want to convey and the topics you want to cover. Some companies focus on their product (like Nike Running), others on the needs of their community and culture (like WeWork).

Content is king but context is queen. When it comes to content strategy, on Instagram, as on any social network, there is no exact rule to follow. It all depends on the context in which you are operating, but above all on your buyer persona, or rather, what your ideal customer might expect to see and interact with.

The most important thing is that you create content that interests and engages your followers, and with which you can achieve your goals.

For this reason, you should first create the foundation on which you can then develop your content.

All companies, regardless of size, industry, or geography, have the opportunity to share quality content on Instagram.

This content can be about the stories of the people in the company, the company culture, the product and its applications, demonstrations, and so on.

The most popular types of content shared by companies are Behind-the-scenes, user-generated content (through re-sharing), product demonstrations and presentations, educational content (guides), cultural content that showcases the brand ethos and values, fun and entertaining content, customer stories, and case studies, and content to showcase the team.

Before deciding on what type of content to focus on, it can be useful to brainstorm ideas and then formulate the content marketing strategy.

Tell a story

The future of marketing on Instagram is about telling a story with your photos.

As with all content, the bar for quality continues to rise on social media. Brands that want to succeed, especially on Instagram, need to prioritize the great over the merely good, even if that means reducing the frequency of posts.

On Instagram, it also helps a lot if your feed tells the same general story through notable content and repetition. If your content goes in many directions, it's very difficult to attract followers who are passionate about a particular topic.

Go ahead and do multiple stories, but make sure they're worth watching

Instagram is flooded with mediocre posts from brands who forget that the social network is supposed to be a 'platform for visual inspiration'.

Intrigue your audience with images, videos and stories, don't just advertise.

Instead, become a storyteller, offer "micro-stories" through captions, videos, Instagram Stories, and Instagram profiles to increase engagement rates.

Authenticity wins

In 2018, Instagram has done a lot to clean up the platform of bots, fake likes, and fake "influencers" and ensure that malicious services selling fake followers have ceased to exist. Furthermore, Instagram is not only fighting against automation apps but also against users who exploit them. If you rely on artificial tools to automate your online presence, some of your Instagram features could be removed as a kind of "punishment" for using bad practices.

Edelman's 2018 Trust Barometer found that 60% of respondents no longer trust social media companies.

Create authentic content, tell stories with your captions, and use Instagram Stories features such as emoji, sliders, gifs, or the question sticker.

Due to Instagram's algorithm, creating beautiful and engaging content is not enough to increase your engagement rate.

You need to implement daily routines that will help you increase engagement. Like, comment and interact with your audience or potential followers, don't just be social, be social. It's important to engage at least 10-30 minutes before and after posting, schedule posts but also comment, share and create Instagram Stories about them.

3 success stories

The mainstays of Saturday Night Live's Instagram profile are behind-the-scenes shots of the show and exclusive clips reserved for followers.

FedEx's Instagram profile focuses on visual content about the vehicles the company uses to make deliveries, such as vans, trucks, and planes. Their feed is a mix of artistic and exciting photo content.

Oreo, on the other hand, focuses on its product through fun and highly engaging content. They often include funny phrases in images and use very colorful and uniform backgrounds to make their posts stand out within the platform.

6 important steps to an effective Instagram content plan.

Once you've defined your topics (but you can always revise them based on the results of your campaigns), it's time to combine them into a content plan.

This will allow you to define the style and design of your posts, as well as the frequency with which you publish content.

To have a consistent profile on Instagram that conveys the right message, it is important to follow a precise style that reflects that of the other marketing channels you use. In this regard, you can create style guides that can be followed when creating content, the main points of which are:

Composition. This refers to the positioning of elements within the visual content and, more generally, the structure of the photo or video. Not all marketers are skilled photographers, so it can be useful to establish some rules regarding the background, the focus of the content, and the space needed for text at the top or bottom of the image.

Colour palette. If you always use the same color palette, you can create a consistent and focused feed. But be careful. Specifying a range of colors to be used does not mean depriving yourself of the possibility of using other colors, but it will help give your content a familiar feel. A good idea is to choose a color palette that matches the colors normally used by the brand in other marketing channels so that users will more easily recognize your business and therefore your brand.

Fonts. If you include quotes or text in the images you post on Instagram, it's important to create consistency through the fonts you use, which should match the rest of your company's communications.

Filters. With these tools, even the most inexperienced photographers can make their photos look great. Filters can drastically change the look of your photos and videos. Therefore, it is important to use only a few (those that best suit your message) to avoid confusing the user. Using a different filter for each post creates confusion and disorientation for your followers, who will not be able to easily recognize your posts.

Captions. Instagram provides more than enough space for image captions; beyond this limit, the text will be cut off. This space allows you to further differentiate your content and take it to the next level. There are several ways to use this space. Some use it for micro-blogging, others use it to include a short catchy title or to ask questions to users. The possibilities are endless. The important thing is to always maintain a certain consistency.

Hashtags. Hashtags have become the most widely used tool on social networks to categorize the content produced and posted. On Instagram, hashtags allow users to discover new content and accounts to follow. If you want to avoid putting too many hashtags in the caption, a good way is to put them in the comments. By analyzing the most popular hashtags used by your users before choosing the most appropriate ones for your content, you can ensure that you reach a wider audience.

Hashtags are extremely important. Like emoji, they are much, much more than a fad used by teenagers. They provide a mechanism for users to quickly navigate along topics of interest by grouping published posts with hyperlinks.

Choosing the best hashtags for your Instagram posts can make all the difference. Make your hashtags too generic - #christmas or #fashion for example - your post will compete with millions of other competitors. Instead, use a mix of trending and industry-specific hashtags to find the best hashtag to reach your followers.

The number of hashtags you distribute is also crucial. Although Instagram allows a maximum of 30, having a mass of hashtags under your caption risks looking unfocused and unprofessional. That's why 91% of top brand posts use seven or fewer hashtags to get lots of likes.

What is the right frequency to post on Instagram?

There's a lot to be said for consistency and coherence when posting on social media.

The consistency and frequency with which you post content can help your audience understand when to expect new content from your business. By maintaining a consistent schedule, you can maximize engagement without taking breaks or extending quiet periods when updates aren't posted.

A study by Union Metrics shows that most brands post daily on Instagram, with an average of 1.5 posts per day, but this number should by no means be taken as an indicator.

The study also shows that there is no correlation between an increase in posting frequency and a decrease in engagement levels, as companies that post more than two twice per day did not see negative results.

How enjoyable is it to have a community just waiting to hear the next thing you have to say?

This creates a planned and relevant publishing schedule. A steady diet of buzz at regular intervals.

It develops content by creating a pipeline of automated posts that are published on a set schedule.

As with a subscription service, this aspect of an effective Instagram strategy becomes crucial. Routines meet users' expectations and build trust by fulfilling their needs.

Think of Instagram posts as seeds you plant, spaced out and in a row.

To generate steady growth, we recommend posting at least two or three pieces of content per day and experimenting with an additional post to see what type of content best fits your reality and the needs of your target audience.

To determine the best time to publish, use a service like Iconosquare or the excellent Co-Schedule.

These powerful tools provide detailed analysis on a variety of aspects, including optimization.

What time to post?

With the recent changes to Instagram's timeline algorithm, timing is one of the elements the platform considers when deciding what content to show users. Therefore, it is important to post during the time intervals when your target audience is most present on Instagram to get more engagement.

According to a study by CoSchedule, the best days to increase engagement on Instagram are Mondays and Thursdays between 8 and 9 a.m. (EST).

Of course, this data comes from extensive research and may not reflect the habits of your target audience. That's why it's so important to find out the habits of your followers on Instagram using the statistics function of your Instagram account. This way you can find out when your followers are most active and plan accordingly to ensure your posts continue to appear at the top of their feeds.

Even if you see that most of your followers are active on Instagram at a certain time (usually mornings and evenings after work 5-6), it doesn't mean that your posts will perform better at that time. This is because it's harder to reach the top of the scrolling feed on your followers' accounts due to increased competition at these times.

Engagement on Instagram is highest at weekends (22.3%), so it may be worth scheduling some posts for Saturday or Sunday.

Posting at the weekend is easy with third-party scheduling solutions, but you also need to find time on Saturday and Sunday to respond to posts and comments.

Once you have determined the topics, posting frequency, and posting times, it makes sense to create an editorial calendar that lists all the content to be posted and the corresponding periods.

Unfortunately, Instagram does not currently offer the ability to schedule posts yourself. However, you can use additional software such as UNUM, Planoly, OnlyPult, Later, Instapult, and TakeOff for this purpose.

A consistently planned editorial program creates anticipation and expectation. This is the key to growth in social media marketing activities and even more so today on Instagram.

Interact with your followers and encourage interactions.

You can simply post your images, but we have observed that success happens when you are proactive.

Invite your followers to interact with your content.

A great way to encourage engagement is to use interactive content. Interactive content engages your audience more, increases click-through rates, and provides more opportunities to inform and engage with your network.

Create any type of action that stimulates user engagement with your content to trigger the algorithm that will subsequently make your content reach as many people as possible.

To do this, you can use open or closed questions, ask people to answer a survey, or ask them something on Instagram stories.

Think of each of your posts as an opportunity to interact with your followers. Give your fans something to do and watch interactions increase like wildfire.

Of course, don't misinterpret this advice - you shouldn't ask your followers for something to do in every post...

Instead, it's important to understand that you don't need to ask them to buy your product, give out their email or share our account with everyone they know every time. It's much more subtle than what you ask for.

You need to ask your followers for something that makes them feel satisfied or reinforces their values or goals.

You can get up to 300% more interaction with this method than with a simple post.

Each post is an opportunity to generate interactions, increase conversions and engage with your community.

Publishing your content should get users to do more than "digest" a photo.

For explosive growth, users must push themselves to share your content.

Every element of your post on Instagram should offer the opportunity to encourage interactions and build your network.

Interactive content helps you increase engagement rates

Also according to this study, engagement on Instagram, as measured by likes, shares, and consumer comments, is 10 times higher than on Facebook, 54 times higher than on Pinterest, and 84 times higher than on Twitter.

How to measure the results of your marketing strategy on Instagram

Monitoring performance and results are essential for any social strategy you implement.
This will help you understand what content is most engaging for your audience and allow you to optimize your strategy in the future.
By paying attention to the growth in the number of followers, likes, and comments on your posts, you can understand what actually works (and therefore bringing results) and what needs to be improved.
Measuring engagement on Instagram is very simple: add the number of likes and comments to your post and divide it by the number of followers you had at the time of the post.
If you want to take more precise measurements, you can opt for ad hoc measurement software. Social media management tools or social CRM tools that can track performance, monitor trends, control hashtag usage, measure user engagement, and manage multiple profiles.
Sentiment analysis tools are also very useful, allowing you to see when users are talking about you and their attitude towards your brand.

6 quick and practical tips to grow and increase engagement on Instagram

Use user-generated content
Instagram users provide your business with a wealth of high-quality content. Curating user-generated content helps you create an active, vibrant community and encourages your audience to share creative content that shows how they interact with your product or service and their relationship with your brand.

Leverage employee-generated content
Employee-created content receives eight times more engagement than content shared by the company itself. What's more, employee content increases brand messaging by over 500%. Your company now needs to engage employees in content creation. It's a known fact that companies with engaged employees outperform their competitors; involving employees in content creation can help create a sense of community.

Adding faces to posts to increase interaction
Georgia Tech analyzed over a million photos on Instagram and found that photos with faces received 38% more likes and 32% more comments.

Better GIFs than photos
The GIF format is more appealing than photos, GIFs are shared more often than JPEG or PNG formats, and are more

expensive and effective than video productions. GIFs inspired Instagram to create Boomerangs, which take a short sequence of still images before combining them and then pushing them back and forth, ready to be uploaded to Instagram. The tool has already seen great results for brands experimenting with the young medium to increase engagement on Instagram.

Convert Instagram followers into email subscribers.
Email remains the channel for building truly deep relationships with customers. That's why brands strive to convert Instagram followers into email subscribers. First, create a clickable incentive in your Instagram posts depending on your target audience. For example, consider offering a prize, free content, or a discount. Once your target audience clicks, make sure your landing page includes a strong call to action linked to an email form. Finally, create a mailing list to effectively engage your new email subscribers so you can start building more meaningful relationships with them.

Share your Instagram posts on Facebook
A study by Buzzsumo of over 1 billion Facebook posts shared by around 3 million business pages found that content shared directly from Instagram gets more engagement than content posted directly on Facebook. Spread the word as much as possible on your Instagram channel. For example, promote your Instagram account on Facebook by creating a Facebook ad with a clickable link to your Instagram page. You can also take advantage of Instagram's self-posting and cross-promotion tools. Cross-promotion tools allow you to instantly

post from Instagram to Facebook, Twitter, Tumblr, and more, bringing your followers together across all social networks. Remember not to promote all your Instagram posts on other social channels or you risk 'cannibalizing' your content and negating the need for followers to visit your Instagram channel in the first place.

Instagram Direct and the rise of the dark social

Since 2018, there has been a surge in the use of Instagram Direct, which has evolved from a simple one-to-one medium to a robust group chat platform with the addition of GIFs, videos, and more recently audio notes. To date, it seems that not only are people using this feature, but it is even becoming a popular alternative to Messenger and WhatsApp.

Thanks to its features, Instagram Direct is making it increasingly easy to start a private conversation and share or copy links with someone on Instagram, and that includes businesses.

So, if you don't have a DM strategy yet, now is the time to think about it. DMs can be great for customer service, humanizing your brand, audience research on Instagram, increasing sales and conversions, and more.

This phenomenon is known as dark social.
Dark social refers to all communication between a company and its target audience (or between users themselves) that

cannot be measured in terms of likes, shares, and comments. However, by using Dark Customer Care, you can better understand the sentiment of your audience and have a direct measure of the level of loyalty of your followers.

How can you use Dark Social to get the best activity on Instagram? We suggest you explore this topic right now with this comprehensive guide

CHAPTER 12

12 TACTICS TO INCREASE SALES THROUGH INSTAGRAM

Marketing on Instagram is not that easy. It requires soft skills and knowledge of a few tools to get started. But the rapid growth of Instagram has also been accompanied by an incredible increase in user interactions.

Studies have shown that brands receive on average 25% more engagement on Instagram than on any other social network. Impressive, isn't it?

This means that Instagram is a great place to increase brand awareness, but also to increase sales. The real million-dollar question is: where can you find marketing tactics that work on Instagram?

Tactic 1
Use advanced influencer marketing
Until a year ago, not everyone knew what the term influencer meant. Today, it has emphatically entered common parlance. Social marketers who have had satisfactory access to

influencers through their use in successful online campaigns are now dealing with much-changed scenarios.

Influencer marketing has taken on many aspects and facets and has truly become an indispensable part of the marketing mix.

If you read on, you will discover the enormous possibilities offered by what could be called the most human and authentic marketing of today, with a few exceptions and clarifications.

Consider that there are over 60,000 influencers on Instagram, covering all vertical markets, including fashion, beauty, health and wellness, home decor, food, and more.

To retain their followers and brand offerings, they expect "authenticity" for 2023. The days of edited posts and photos and bot comments on Instagram are over, making way for more authentic experiences and relationships.

Connecting your brand with influencers who genuinely love your product and are happy to share it with their followers is an ideal way to build an authentic relationship on Instagram and drive better engagement and results.

Adding Instagram influencer marketing to your overall Instagram strategy can help you increase your brand awareness, grow your follower base and generate more sales. Influencer marketing on Instagram has become increasingly important these days. It allows marketers to collaborate with thought leaders and industry experts to get the brand message across to a wider audience.

According to a Nielsen report, 92% of consumers trust the recommendations of individuals (even if they don't know them) more than brands. Using trustworthy, reputable, and likable of people is a great strategy to market your brand.

The future of marketing on Instagram will increasingly focus on influencer relationships and engagement.

As influencers are considered 'independent', aligning your brand with their authoritative voice can add authenticity to your message.

Algorithms continue to favor people over brands, and the challenges of creating authentic and engaging visual content for users in the face of competition means that using influencers is your insurance policy for continuing to be heard on Instagram.

However, choosing the right influencer can be difficult.

Plan an influencer strategy that includes a short trial period to see how receptive the follower network of the influencer you've chosen specifically for your brand is.

You also need to ensure that your influencer is given the tools, resources, and guidance they need to play their role effectively, that they work side by side with you on the campaign as a true partner.

New collaboration strategies are increasing the impact of social media

In 2018, there has been an interesting trend on Instagram that has begun to redefine how brands collaborate with influencers.

While previously most brands would send products to influencers and expect to see a sponsored post in their feed and Stories, brands are now considering sending influencers on vacation.

The premise is simple: select the most influential influencers on Instagram with millions of followers, send them to a luxury hotel to relax, let them try out products, and, of course, have them post all about it.
This is how fashion brands like Revolve or Boohoo have taken small groups of Instagram's most-followed influencers on vacation and taken advantage of their followers in successful campaigns.
The strategy is to curate and coordinate image-rich content in postcard-ready locations, as well as raw shots showing the brand from other angles.

The tactic is to prepare an exciting adventure, with Instagram-worthy meals and other offline experiences, so that influencers can show how the product or service fits into the perfect lifestyle to which the influencer's followers aspire. Of course, the inclusion of purchase links in influencer content should not be ignored.
Such a campaign, if well prepared, costs a lot of money.
However, the ads you create are not short 30-second TV spots, but a series of posts and stories that leave a much longer impact on the brand. You can also promote your brand's hashtag, harness the power of user-generated content and reuse footage for a campaign.

Work with influencers who are more authentic and therefore more sumptuous for the brand.

"Authenticity" is another Instagram marketing "trend" that is very valid in 2022.

Gone are the days of Instagram posts with perfect poses, over-edited photos, and Instagram bot comments, giving way to authentic experiences and relationships?

2018 saw the rise of a new generation of Instagram influencers who focus on authenticity, such as Jenna Kutcher, who gained over half a million followers in one year and went from 166 to 700k+ without ever paying for a single follower. The influencer marketing industry has exploded thanks to Instagram and global influencer advertising spend is expected to reach $5-10 billion by 2022.

While brands are excited about influencer marketing, regular Instagram users are starting to see beyond the perfect sponsored posts.

To retain their followers and partnerships with brands, Instagram influencers are expected to become more personal and authentic in 2023. This includes conversations about sponsored content, with influencers reaching out to thank their followers for supporting their sponsored posts and explaining how much of their income comes from their business.

The influencers of 2023 build their success by continually demonstrating their increased transparency and authenticity on Instagram, showing that they actually consume their sponsored brands' products, buy and repurchase them, and even go so far as to show off their empty packaging. This simple gesture could represent the new breed of influencer, more trustworthy and authentic, more valuable to brands.

Even brands are starting to give hints of authenticity.

One of the best ways to create authentic brand partnerships is to think long-term. Think about the influencers you work with as brand ambassadors and sign contracts that last more than a year and include multiple posts per month.

Connecting your brand with influencers who genuinely love your product and enthusiastically share it with their followers is an ideal way to build an authentic relationship on Instagram.

When influencers consistently post with your brand over a long period, it not only increases brand recall but helps followers connect your brand with the influencer, which can lead to better engagement and results.

Micro and nano influencers for the best engagement rates.

Bigger isn't always better when it comes to marketing on Instagram, a reality that many celebrity influencers are facing as brands are starting to work with micro-influencers (accounts that have less than 100,000 followers).

"Nano-influencers" are also on the rise as brands choose to work with average users with a follower base of 1,000 for sponsored posts and branded campaigns.

Nano-influencers are a secret weapon for social media marketers. Nano-influencers have a following of around

5,000 followers, but they have a niche following. They represent the typical geeky friend who is good at social networking.

Although their following is much smaller than that of a celebrity, their community is more engaged.

Two separate studies by HelloSociety and Markerly found that influencers with smaller numbers of followers had much higher engagement rates than influencers with larger numbers of followers, and both studies found a decline in engagement rates as audience size increased.

According to a Digiday survey, nano-influencers can engage up to 8.7% of their followers, while the engagement rate of famous influencers with more than one million followers is only 1.7%.

Working with influencers with smaller accounts is not only cheaper but can also be more effective.

These types of nano-influencer and micro-influencer marketing campaigns will take off in 2022 as brands make more use of authenticity and the algorithm.

But it's not just influencers who will benefit from smaller, highly engaged audiences in 2022; micro-brands are also on the rise.

Micro-brands are no different to a small business, there is nothing 'small' about them.

Micro-brands on Instagram compete with large retailers and can generate millions of dollars in sales with small teams through the power of their data-driven design and the low cost of customer acquisition via social media.

Thanks to the hyper-targeting capabilities of Instagram ads, micro-brands can design and sell products created for a very specific customer, which they can then target on Instagram.

Big brands are becoming aware of their smaller competitors and are responding by creating their in-house micro-brands.

These examples also show that people want personalized and targeted content and are quick to click the unfollow button if they disagree with the content in your feed.

If you want to retain Instagram followers in 2023, create targeted content for your ideal customer. Use your Instagram analytics to see what content resonates best and if the demographics of your Instagram followers match those of your customers.

Tactic #2

Use Instagram to maximize your brand positioning with storytelling.

The best way to position a brand is to tell a story that people want to hear, right? And what better way to tell a story than with visual content? Our brains are 'wired' to understand images 60,000 times faster than text. This means that people are more likely to understand your message if you use images in your strategy.

This is where Instagram comes to the rescue. As you probably know, Instagram is 100% visual. Every brand needs a story that differentiates its products from other brands, and

Instagram is the best social network for sharing visual content.

By posting images that support any kind of storytelling about your brand, you can get better position yourself in the minds of your target audience.

Tactic #3

Use hashtags wisely to increase engagement

Twitter may have invented social media hashtags, but Instagram has really mastered them and now a hashtag strategy on Instagram delivers many results.

Choosing the best hashtags for your posts on Instagram can mean the difference between looking like a top post or sinking to the bottom of the feed without a trace.

Nowadays, Instagram hashtags not only categorize content and make it discoverable for users, but they are also an effective way to gain more followers, increase engagement and expand reach and brand awareness.

Make your hashtags too generic and your post will compete with millions of others. Instead, use a mix of trending and industry-specific hashtags to find the best hashtag to connect with your targeted followers.

If you want to harness the platform's potential to reach a large audience, increase the role of hashtags on Instagram.

According to a study by Agorapulse, Instagram posts with at least one hashtag received 70% more likes and 392% more comments than those without hashtags.

As organic reach decreases and paid impressions increase with the introduction of algorithms that force brands to pay for their presence, hashtags are still the best way to organically drive your social marketing campaigns by using Instagram posts to increase reach on the platform.
Dive into hashtag research.

It's important to research hashtags before you use them, because the more relevant and targeted the hashtags are, the greater the chances of reaching an audience that will interact with the content you post.
Depending on your goals, there are many types of research you can do to find the best possible Instagram hashtags. Here are the most effective techniques:

1. search for relevant topics.
A good place to start is by researching trends related to your industry. The keywords you use in the SEO of your website could be a good starting point for your hashtag search.
In the Instagram app, tap the magnifying glass icon, then select 'hashtags' and type the words one by one into the Instagram search bar.
The results of each search will show all the best hashtags that are closely related to the hashtag you're searching for, and

give you ideas for even more hashtags you can use to reach and connect with your audience.

Scroll through your search results regularly and then browse through posts that contain Instagram hashtags to keep an eye on them and remember hashtag trends that might be used in future posts.

2. research your target audience.

Instead of posting generic hashtags, take a more targeted approach to grow your following by finding out what hashtags your audience is currently using or searching for. Look beyond the numbers by avoiding overuse hashtags.

Think specifically, because in general, the lower the reach of a particular hashtag, the more likely users are to engage with the topics posted with that hashtag.

For even more targeted engagement, go deeper by experimenting with the long-tail hashtags your audience is searching for.

3. Research your industry experts.

One of the most effective ways to find the hashtags you should use is to follow influencers and companies on Instagram that share your audience to see what hashtags they're using. You'll probably discover some new hashtags to add to your arsenal.

Find the top brands in your industry and compete directly with them using the same industry-specific Instagram hashtags.

More tips for researching potential Instagram hashtags.

Do a Google search for your hashtag without the "#" symbol with and without spaces between words.

Use a hashtag search tool to identify powerful hashtags.

Search Instagram, Twitter, Facebook, and other social platforms to see if your hashtag has been used.

Make sure your hashtag doesn't have a second meaning that could confuse your potential audience.

Check all acronyms you use in hashtags for possible double meanings.

Check your spelling for accuracy before posting.

Use Instagram hashtags selectively

There are many studies on how many hashtags to use in each post to increase engagement.

Depending on which study you rely on, the best number of hashtags ranges from five to the maximum allowed of 30.

An analysis by TrackMaven found that using 11 hashtags in each post is optimal for increasing engagement on Instagram. The reality is that the key to successful Instagram hashtags is to use them strategically, whether you choose three deeply researched hashtags or 30 carefully selected ones.

Being as specific as possible with your hashtags also narrows the pool of targeted users, making it easier to build a highly engaged audience.

Add hashtags to your Instagram profile bio for conversations and shares.

Since the Instagram bio only allows for a standard hyperlink, adding hashtags encourages people to start conversations and share experiences around your brand.

Instagram hashtags can now be embedded in profiles, a feature that provides an extra boost by linking to the hashtag feed. However, don't expect your bio to be discoverable in hashtag search results.

Add "#" in front of any word in your profile and it automatically becomes a clickable link that can be used for anything, such as promoting the Instagram community you create.

Use special daily hashtags to activate and inspire your content.

Daily hashtags provide a way to engage with your audience daily, keeping them constantly engaged with your content and connecting with them over the long term. In Italy, daily hashtags are almost all adopted from English.

Use a balanced mix of general, niche, and location-based hashtags.

Include a brand hashtag in every Instagram post. Use a campaign hashtag.

Hide hashtags to make posts more engaging in the feed.

To keep readers focused on your well-written caption, it's advisable to minimize the flashy appearance of your Instagram hashtag list, as it comes across as cluttered, spammy, or out of place in posts.

You can hide hashtags using one of two methods:

In captions:
After ending the caption with a full stop, press "Enter".
Type a full stop or a dash, then press enter again and repeat four times
Enter your hashtags after the last line

In the comments:
Post your content, as usual, making sure to leave the hashtags out of the caption
Once you've published your post, click on the cartoon icon below to leave a comment
Enter your hashtags in the "Add a comment..." box and then tap "Publish".
After your post has received multiple comments, the hashtags will no longer be visible

Instagram hides captions after three lines, so your hashtags won't be visible unless your followers tap the "More" option or read the comments on your post.
Adding hashtags to Instagram Stories to build a new audience
Adding hashtags to Instagram Stories, whether in the form of text, a sticker, or a location tag, gives your content another way to be found by a new audience.
However, adding hashtags to images or videos on Instagram Stories is no guarantee of reaching large chunks of new audiences, as it all depends on the quality of the content you post and the level of engagement. The risk is worth it, as these features are still underused by brands on Instagram.

All you need to do is add a hashtag or location sticker to your posts on Instagram Stories.

Organize or attend a live event. Whether it's a conference, an event, or a holiday, this is the time when people are busiest seeing what's happening in real-time on Instagram. So making your story visible to others is a great way to attract new eyes to your Instagram profile and gain more followers.

When your story is added to the location story, you usually get a notification from Instagram. If a photo or video from your Story is visible on a hashtag or location page, you'll see the name of that page when you see who has viewed your Story.

If you go to your Instagram explorer page, you'll see the live Story for the city you're in, but your Story will only have the option to be displayed if you add a location sticker to your Instagram Stories.

As well as using the same hashtags you use in standard posts, there are a few other ways to do this:

1. use location tags.

Instagram stories appear on Instagram's Discover page, which means that even people who don't follow you can find and see your stories.

As well as appearing on the Discover page, your story can also appear in stories for different locations and hashtags.

Research has shown that posts with location tags receive 79% more engagement than those without a geographic tag.

When it comes to Instagram Stories, location tags work almost the same way as traditional hashtags.

There are just a few differences. Locations can only be posted with tags (no text allowed). Each photo or video can only have one location tag.

When tagging locations, such as specific neighborhoods, tagged stories can reach a local, state, regional and national audience.

Location tagging is a great way to promote local businesses or increase visibility in a specific area, especially when Instagram incorporates it into location-based Stories in the Explore feed.

2. Use tags to expand your reach.

Most Instagram geo-locations and hashtags also have their own stories. This way, you can see all recent posts that have been published with a location or hashtag, even if you don't know that user or follow their account.

Positioned creatively, Instagram hashtags can be used as an effective tool to grow your audience by engaging followers and touching their friends.

Follow people who have already liked or followed your brand and see the hashtags they use in their posts and stories, then use the same tags.

Take advantage of niches, branded hashtags, and events.

Instagram hashtags come in many varieties and each has its uses and target audience. Here's what you need to know about the main types of custom tags to define an effective strategy:

1. niche hashtags

You can use niche hashtags to connect your brand with a specific audience that is most likely to engage and do business with you.

To reach a highly targeted audience, use very specific niche hashtags that offer a greater chance of visibility and conversions.

2. branded/personalized hashtags.

These hashtags are unique, created by you, for your brand on Instagram and are a great way to increase awareness of your business and give your followers a way to interact with you and each other.

A branded hashtag can be something as simple as your company name, slogan, or brand identity, or it could be linked to specific products, services, or marketing campaigns.

Branded hashtags increase brand awareness and allow your customers to share relevant content.

3. event hashtags

Event-specific hashtags are used to direct attendees, visitors, and customers to real events, venues, and local attractions to increase engagement.

Make event hashtags relevant, descriptive, short, and easy to understand. Then make sure you use them before, during, and after the event. Finally, don't forget to use event hashtags in offline promotions to drive traffic to your social channels.

Use hashtags from themed channels to reach an untapped audience.

Themed channels, located at the top of the Explore section, are a relatively new way for users to browse different categories of the published content.

These recommended channels vary based on user behavior on the platform and display Instagram hashtags related to the channel being viewed.

Since Instagram considers these hashtags important enough to display, it's a safe bet that its members will use and search for them.

Channel hashtags are especially useful for connecting with unreached members of your target audience. So use the hashtags displayed in themed channels in your posts to increase their awareness and reach.

Use hashtags to build communities around your brand.

Find ways to use ultra-niche hashtags to target and engage an active community to increase your brand's visibility and engagement while creating a conversation about your business. Micro-communities are also relevant.

To find community-oriented hashtags, do some research and see what Instagram hashtags your target audience uses when talking about things related to your brand and then adopt them.

To create a community, give users and consumers an incentive (a freebie or downloadable content) to use the hashtag.

Avoid banned hashtags to avoid censorship.

To keep the platform's content in line with its terms of service, Instagram bans certain hashtags, so they can't appear in search results.

Although there is no comprehensive list of banned Instagram hashtags, Instagram bans hashtags related to violence, insults, pornography, organized crime, and terrorism.

Instagram also bans several hashtags for their misuse, even if they are harmless.

To find out if the hashtags you use are banned, click on the magnifying glass icon on the Explore page. Enter the target hashtag in the search bar. If the hashtag does not appear in the search results, it will be banned (temporarily or permanently). Banned hashtags can still appear in search results, so click on them if they are banned, a link to an incorrect page will be displayed.

If your posts receive less engagement (likes and comments) or do not appear in search, you may be in a shadowban status. A shadowban prevents your Instagram posts from being shown to any users who don't follow you, which can hinder your growth.

To avoid a shadowban, avoid illegal hashtags, automated third-party apps that rely on hashtags.

4. monitor hashtag performance

If you have an Instagram business profile, you can measure the effectiveness of your hashtags and use the data to improve your strategy to get more views and engagement.

Tracking the hashtag performance of each of your posts will help you better focus your strategy.

To access this valuable feature, open any post and then tap on the "View stats" text below the photo.

Then scroll up to see the full details of the post, including followers, reach and impressions, and how users discovered the post.

Although Instagram Insights limits the period in which you can view metrics to 7 days for regular posts and 14 days for Stories, some third-party apps can provide more in-depth data.

It's important to continually track, analyze, experiment, and test which hashtags are attracting new followers and increasing engagement.

Tactic #4.

Cross-promote to grow your followers faster.

Most users and brands don't do this, but cross-promotion (or simply co-marketing) is one of the most effective ways to grow your following on any social network.

You can ask a stakeholder to tell their followers about you and to follow you so that you can do the same for them.

The problem is that this practice became practically spam at first, but now things have definitely changed and if this kind of co-marketing is done elegantly, it can be effective.

The biggest mistake when it comes to cross-promotion is sending requests to the wrong people.

To avoid wasting time, it is very effective to exchange a few messages before the actual launch and make sure you present yourself naturally and with a direct and clear message.

We can't forget about Instagram pods

In recent years, the fashion for Instagram Pods, also called Instagram Engagement Pods, has exploded. These are groups (public or private) where users try to trick Instagram's algorithm to get more followers, likes, comments, and views. The goal of such groups is to increase engagement of one's Instagram profile by having real, active users who exchange likes on posts and possibly leave a comment.

There are several ways to join Instagram pods: Some are public and require no special rules, while others are private and require an invitation from one of the group members.

The benefits are certainly immediate. The increase in engagement is quick, just take the time to like all the pod members and hope they reciprocate.

The disadvantages?

Of course, this practice is not without its pitfalls. Firstly, engagement rates can be skewed and even fall off quickly if not practiced continuously.

So weigh up all the pros and cons and then decide if Instagram pods groups are right for you to grow on Instagram.

Tactic #5

Use bridge marketing to increase sales

Have you ever heard of bridge marketing? It's when you create a bridge between your business and a specific niche so that more people can be attracted to your products or services. For example, let's say you're starting a business in industrial lighting and you're looking for specialist designers to work with.

While this type of user is browsing, they might come across an "ad" on Instagram advertising "We specialize in industrial lighting, learn more here".

It's all about segmenting your ad campaigns on Instagram and creating tailored ads for each segment.

As with Facebook, the more specific the segments you create (thanks to segmentation by gender, location, age, niche), the more useful the messages you can leverage for your audience.

Tactic #6

Use video to communicate your brand

Most brands have now embraced video marketing and the frequency of video posts on Instagram has gradually increased over the last few years.

Video marketing on Instagram is an opportunity for a business to show the world who they are and what they do in the space of a minute or less.

People want connections, the personalization of the relationship has come down to face to face with your followers, whether it's Instagram Stories, Instagram TV, or a good old video post.

One of the dictates of the moment is to explore the full range of video formats on Instagram

A picture may be worth a thousand words, but a video is worth millions. There is no comparison to the effectiveness and popularity of online video content.

Instagram has recognized this and offers a range of video options that are very attractive to marketers.

For example, consider the "live video" option of Instagram Stories to showcase new products or services, or use a pre-recorded ad to give your followers authentic behind-the-scenes stories to communicate branding and increase engagement on Instagram.

Less curated videos work better on Instagram Stories

For a long time, brands have been posting very sophisticated videos on Instagram to attract customers. Producing these videos takes time and financial investment, and Instagram's algorithm won't let you capture the results of the platform's early days.

Today, however, it is the less curated but truer videos, which take less time to create and publish, that perform better on Instagram. Instagram users, for the most part, are not interested in seeing highly curated videos. Preferences have changed over time, but they are looking for content that is authentic and relevant to them.

Invite your employees and executives to talk freely about their challenges, promote products or services in videos.

Use video captions in Instagram stories

With the increasing dominance of online videos, especially on mobile devices, audio has become less important and most users prefer not to have sound on while watching a video. This is why subtitles have become so important to marketers, as they allow basic messages to be conveyed on screen alongside images.

Research from Facebook shows that video subtitles increase the average time spent watching videos by 12%. There has also been a massive increase in the effectiveness of messaging. The success rate was 82% compared to 18% with audio enabled and no subtitles.

Automatic subtitle insertion is offered by Facebook, but beware of mistakes) alternatively, you can create your subtitle file, which is more or less simply inserted into the video track.

Use Instagram's video ad formats to sell and communicate your brand.

With 75% of followers claiming to take actions such as visiting websites, researching, or seeking advice from a friend after being influenced by a post, mastering the platform's various ad formats is crucial.

While photo ads remain a staple of the platform, Instagram's video formats are an important tool for targeting select audiences.

There are three video formats for creating Instagram ads:

'single video ads' offer the ability to create ads up to 60 seconds long
'Carousels' offer multiple scrolling messages
Instagram story videos offer a full-screen vertical format where images and videos can be combined to create visually engaging ads.

Instagram TV: What you need to know to get started
IGTV is a standalone vertical video app and, unlike Instagram, videos are not limited to one minute, but can be up to an hour long. In this way, Instagram is ending the traditional TV experience and updating it for a modern mobile experience.

Instagram is banking on the popularity of its video content and has decided to launch an app that will allow influencers, brands, and organizations a new way to communicate with their followers through a video in a vertical format.
The idea almost certainly wouldn't have been successful if we hadn't become accustomed to the vertical videos of IG Stories, which have become so popular that the move to IGTV was something that made sense.

YouTube is incredibly popular with kids and teens, and IGTV is Instagram's hope for a piece of that video popularity pie. Many publishers have seen their repurposed YouTube videos get millions of views on IGTV.

Instagram's IGTV could have a future where it is no longer about exclusive content but could become one of the default channels for video marketing: with less competition for views and a unique, mobile-optimized layout perfect for experimenting with shots and perspectives.

Instagram is still growing fast and has a very engaged user base. Therefore, IGTV may find its niche with exclusive series, influencer vlogs, and experimental video verticals.

Improving video production for Instagram can help you improve the performance of your content in 2023. You don't need to be a pro, just start playing around with apps like InShot or Stereo and post the results to Stories. As you improve, incorporate more vertical videos into your feed.

Tactic #7

Use analytics tools to identify content that generates the most interactions

One of the biggest mistakes people make when managing social media is posting content that you "think" will be of interest. Yes, sometimes you get lucky and people react very positively to your content, but most of the time this doesn't work.

It is much more effective to share photos or videos that have proven successful.

Start by making a list of the 20 most popular Instagram profiles in your industry. Using a tool like SimplyMeasured, you can create a simple spreadsheet of 'top posts'.

By analyzing the information, you can make some very interesting leads and suggestions by looking at what they have in common.

What kind of content are they sharing?
How often are they sharing it?
What kind of filters are they using?
What kind of language do they use?
By paying attention to these elements, you will be able to shape the start-up and development of a new content strategy and get better results.

Tactic #8
Start on Instagram and end on Facebook
If there are still a few people promoting certain products or services on Instagram, it means there are still great opportunities.
Case in point? The Iconic, an Australian fashion and footwear eCommerce company, after launching a campaign on Instagram to increase awareness of its brand among Australian women and drive sales of its new collections, launched a campaign on Facebook the following week targeting the interests and demographics that generated the most interactions on Instagram.
The result? Women who viewed the campaign on both Instagram and Facebook converted 23% more than other active campaigns.

The Instagram campaigns increased brand awareness and drove purchase intent, while the targeted Facebook ads drove people to complete the purchase.

In summary? Launching visually appealing campaigns on Instagram to increase brand awareness and then continuing the campaign via direct ads to increase sales via Facebook is a great way to get the most out of your advertising efforts.

As you can see, Instagram can be an extremely engaging tool that can generate sales if you know how to use it properly.

Tactic #9
Guide users through the conversion funnel
Instagram-marketing-guide-strategy
For most brands, gaining a large number of followers is important, but it's only one step in the overall marketing funnel.

To drive users further down the conversion funnel, you should consider every opportunity to capture your followers' email. And one of the best ways to capture these emails is to request them.

Share an image with a call to action and include a link in the caption about how to download an eBook or sign up for your newsletter.

Once the user has been activated in this way, you can proceed step by step to fully convert them by continuing in other ways (through marketing automation or one-to-one relationship marketing actions).

However, this requires the creation of a targeted and customized landing page. From there, you can then push users through your various channels and keep them updated with your products or services.

Tactic #10
Mix video and photos
Instagram marketing strategy guide
One of the hottest trends in Instagram marketing is to mix photos and videos into your strategy.
Considering that a video can generate three times more shares than a picture-only post, a video is a valuable tool that can be used to engage followers and increase your following and therefore traffic to your website.
Take a look at Oreo or McDonald's on Instagram, for example, and you'll see impressive examples of stop-motion videos that use a product to create entertaining and often incredible storytelling.
Videos can be fun, shareable, and engaging, and with Instagram's video editing features, you can create great results with ease.
For example, with stop motion, you can simply hold down the record button and pause when you want to record another scene. Or you can simply upload a video you've already created.

Tactic #11

Run competitions on Instagram

Instagram marketing contest

Contests are a powerful engagement tool on Instagram. They generate 3.5 times more engagement and 64 times more comments than regular posts.

Yet they are regularly overlooked by brands: only 2% run contests. This means there's a huge, relatively untapped resource for marketers to tap into.

Running a competition on Instagram requires planning a strategy, setting goals and rules, and creating posts that grab attention.

The most common is 'repost' competitions, where the prize in the event of winning is a repost of the winning profile on the social and web channels of the competition organizer, in this case, an appeal to people's visibility and egos. Alternatively, it is also possible to opt for prize competitions offering cash prizes or prizes of a certain amount: we are often talking about weekends in luxury hotels or shopping vouchers.

Tactic #12

Shop on Instagram Instagram shopping

If you run an e-commerce business, you should take advantage of one of the new features available on Instagram: the Shopping function. This feature allows you to add tags to your posts, which means that followers can "tap" the image to see all the information they need to buy a product, such as a price, the name of the item, and the link to the e-commerce page.

This year, a new feature like "Shopping in Stories" helped advertisers put the icon, the shopping bag, on any product or service they promote.
With this option, merchants have the opportunity to target their audience so that they click on the shopping bag icon and see the product image, information, and a link to the website to purchase the product.

With over 400 million users using Instagram Stories every day, advertisers can use this marketing feature to engage with their target customers.
Instagram not only allows shoppable posts in feeds but also shoppable stickers in Stories and a new standalone shopping app could be coming to Instagram soon.

The idea that users can go from inspiration to action with one click and buy directly without leaving the Instagram app is a win-win opportunity for brands, Instagram, and shoppers.
At the moment, only around 20% of marketers are actively using shoppable posts, with the vast majority admitting they have yet to see an increase in sales from shoppable tags.
However, unstoppability remains a trending target on Instagram. Over 50% of Instagram marketers plan to use more shoppable posts in 2023.

The future of marketing is on Instagram, as many Instagram users follow brands (around 80% of users follow at least one brand on Instagram).

Instagram seems to have accepted the challenge of becoming a mainstay of the online shopping experience. Brands and retailers can use shopping features to allow their followers to purchase items directly on the platform.

Many elements can lead to this important strategic conclusion.

Instagram is also increasingly focusing on brands with the introduction of deeper data analytics that are useful for businesses to adjust their activities when introducing shopping features on the platform.

Shopify, with more than 500,000 merchants, is helping eTailers expand their offerings on Instagram's shopping features.

Starting in 2019, you'll be able to shop on Instagram not only from posts and stories in your feed but also from Explore posts and videos. Plus, you can have your own "Shopping" collection on Instagram for easy navigation.

Instagram's shopping features will be a big part of the platform in 2023. So look for opportunities to use direct-to-consumer sales as part of your overall marketing strategy on Instagram.

PART III – INSTAGRAM BUSINESS 2023

CHAPTER 13

11 TRENDS FOR 2023

Marketing on Instagram used to be limited to branded posts and content, then came the era of influencer marketing, and finally, brands found another format to market themselves with Instagram Stories.

Due to the dynamic nature of Instagram marketing and the platform itself, it is difficult to gauge how it will evolve in the future.

Below we have listed the 11 key trends that will shape the future of Instagram marketing in 2023 and most likely beyond.

1. The rise of shopping on Instagram

In recent years, Instagram has established itself as one of the leading online sales platforms. It's not just limited to brands adding direct links to their eShop in their posts, but there is a whole community of online sellers selling exclusively through Instagram.

The visual style of the platform makes it easy for brands to showcase their products and connect with potential customers.

Below are some trends that will drive buying options on Instagram in 2023:

Direct links within Instagram Stories

In 2017, Instagram introduced a feature that allowed direct links to be added to Stories. Since then, many brands have taken advantage of this feature to add direct links to their shop. This trend will continue to grow as it allows brands to showcase their products and increase sales.

The rise of Instagram boutiques

Many Instagram boutiques have emerged, using Instagram as a virtual boutique to showcase their products and facilitate purchases. Instagram's visual style allows products to be displayed virtually, and the right hashtags help brands reach their target audience.

2. Vertical videos

With the increasing use of mobile phones to access social networks or simply to browse, the emergence of vertical video was inevitable. While this video format was rather unpopular, Instagram managed to make it trendy among its users.

The vertical video format is supported by Instagram Live and Instagram Stories as well as IGTV, and because it is a mobile-friendly format, many Instagram users are pushing this trend.

Brands are using this format for a variety of purposes. Whether you want to showcase your products, launch a contest/challenge or show a tutorial, vertical videos can be used for everything.

Best of all, creating a vertical video is easy: just hold your phone vertically.... and start recording!

3. Instagram Stories will continue to grow in popularity

Since launching in 2016, Instagram Stories have been an important part of Instagram marketing. Brands have used the Stories feature in countless creative ways and will continue to do so.

Instagram Stories has become an important aspect of any marketer's Instagram marketing strategy. And with the addition of filters, stickers, and other visual effects, Stories are now more engaging than ever before.

Below are some of the many ways you can use Stories for your marketing on Instagram:

For ads and promotions

Many brands use Instagram Stories to promote their offers, giveaways, competitions, or even just video ads. The ephemeral nature of Stories develops a sense of urgency, which is ideal for promoting offers and giveaways.

Stories are short and engaging, making them an effective medium for brand announcements and promotions.

Conduct a survey or competition

Running a poll or contest on your brand's Instagram Stories is a great way to engage your audience.

You can use polls to gather consumers' opinions and understand their preferences towards your brand or products. Surveys can also be used to get ideas on what customers expect from your brand.
Giving your customers a choice and involving them in the process does wonder for the loyalty of any brand.

You can also use Stories to launch a competition and reward the best entries. This is another proven way to get your customers to engage with your brand.

To announce new product launches.
You can also use Instagram Stories to announce new product launches or simply showcase products.

4.Influencer marketing
Collaborations between brands and influencers will continue to be the backbone of Instagram's marketing strategies for most marketers. And the fact that influencer content is seen as more authentic than branded content will be the key factor in this trend.
Brands are putting more pressure on influencers to create posts, generate links for their websites, and increase consumer engagement and sales. Whether you're promoting a business

or product, or simply looking to generate quality content, influencers can help.

Influencer marketing is also much cheaper than traditional advertising campaigns. Instagram micro-influencers charge between $75 and $3,000 per post, depending on engagement and number of followers. This is still cheaper than the thousands of dollars brands spend on traditional advertising.

Two of the trending ways brands are working with influencers are:

Promoting hashtag campaigns through a network of influencers.

Nowadays, many brands use a network of influencers to promote their Instagram campaigns with specific hashtags. So the idea is to create a specific hashtag for the campaign and promote it in all forms such as stories, posts, highlights, and influencer content.

Attract influencer content by hosting influencer events.

This is a recent trend where some brands invite their influencers to one of their events/trips where everything is paid for by the company. The influencers in turn post about the event, mentioning and promoting the brand.

5. Tweets and memes

In recent years, humorous content has been increasingly posted on Instagram, with some accounts exclusively posting such content. Tweets and memes have become the most popular type of humorous content on Instagram and this trend will continue to grow in 2023.

Marketers are taking advantage of this trend and using this content to their advantage.

You can use your tweets or someone else's. Instagram is all about sharing quality content, so you don't have to create new content every time. This strategy saves you time.

6. Instagram Live will gain popularity

Since the launch of Instagram Live in 2016, live videos have become very popular on the platform. Streaming videos in real-time has several advantages that no other form of content has.

For example, it allows you to interact with your audience in real-time and enables two-way communication, rather than just one-way content sharing. Users can comment and ask questions that can be answered immediately. Instagram Live also allows you to add another user to your live video feed and interact with them live.

This provides many opportunities for your business to engage with your audience. You can use live video to host a Q&A session with your audience, where you can answer their questions. This also provides a great opportunity to understand your customers' concerns and gain valuable insights.

Another great way to use Instagram Live is to interview an industry expert or influencer. They can cover trending topics in your niche that might interest your audience. This is a great way to engage and add value to your audience.

Here are some other ideas to help you take advantage of this trend and use Instagram Live for your business:

Introduce a live product on Instagram and create a buzz about it before making it available on your website. This will help you increase sales.

Go live at a brand event and share the experience with your Instagram followers, even if it's from afar.

Use a live video to demonstrate how to use your product in different ways. A live product tutorial is better than a regular video because it gives your audience a chance to ask questions and seek clarification.

7. Interactive content

Just like live videos, other forms of interactive content are also trending on Instagram. Many brands and marketers are experimenting with interactive content to encourage audience engagement.

Instagram Stories is especially good for creating and sharing interactive content with your audience. Here are some ways to make your content interactive on Instagram:

Ask questions

This is a simple but effective way to make your Instagram content interactive. Simply ask your audience a question and challenge them to answer it. The more responses you get, the better it is for your business.

For posts, you could add an image with a question and ask people to post their answers in the comments. With Instagram Stories, it's much easier because you can ask questions and your followers can answer in the box within your story.

Create a poll

Polls are another popular form of interactive content on Instagram that you can use. They are similar to questions, but with two answer options for participants to choose from.

It's very easy to create polls with Instagram Stories stickers, just like questions. You can insert your poll question and answer options and post them in your Story.

Here are some other ideas you can do to create interactive content on Instagram:

Create a quiz and give your audience a chance to test their knowledge.

Start a countdown to a post, product launch, event, or anything else

Experiment with other interactive Instagram Stories stickers

8. Instagram Stories ads

Instagram Stories ads appear between Stories in a user's feed and can often be mistaken for personal content. As a result, they work much better than other types of ads that stand out as sponsored or branded content.

Marketers have recognized this opportunity and are investing in Instagram Stories ads more than ever before. This trend is set to increase in 2023, which is why you should invest in them if you haven't already.

You can create three different types of ads on Instagram Stories: Images, videos, and carousels. In carousel ads, you can add 3 images or videos in an ad.

Here are some best practices for creating and running Instagram Stories ads that work:

Always include CTAs (call-to-action) in your Instagram Stories ads to direct users to your website.

Make sure the ad is simple and easy to understand, as it will only be visible for a few seconds. It should be such that people immediately understand what your ad is about

Keep text content to a minimum and add images to grab the attention of your audience

Reuse your influencer content and turn it into an ad

Clearly highlight offers or discounts in your ad

If your ad contains only one product, mention the price and add a high-quality image to get more clicks

9. *Explore categories*

If you want to explore new content on Instagram or find new accounts to follow, go to the Explore tab. This will give you content based on your previous history.

Until recently, this was a bit generic, giving you a range of posts you might have liked. Now, however, finding new content has been made easier with the addition of categories. Instead of just getting a list of suggested posts, you can now search for content in categories.

For example, if you like looking at cute animal photos and videos, you might see a category called "Animals", or if you like posts with travel photography, you might find a category called "Travel" in your Explore tab.

As a marketer, you can leverage this category by optimizing your Instagram profile and content to rank higher in these categories. Just as there is SEO for regular searches, there will soon be SEO for Instagram searches.

To benefit from this trend, choose your niche and start optimizing your profile and content with keywords and hashtags from that niche.

If you use the right hashtags, your content will appear in the Explore tab under the relevant categories.

10. Hidden likes to make your content stand out more.

Moving away from the competitive and demanding nature that has developed on the platform, Instagram is returning to its roots with a focus on creativity, spontaneity, and storytelling.

'No-edit' editing was a big trend in 2022, and it doesn't seem to be going anywhere in 2023 either. The focus is on minimal editing of photos to achieve a more authentic look.

This trend is good news for video content too! You no longer need to spend thousands of dollars on the sophisticated, high-quality video to reap the rewards: By 2023, you'll see a lot more video in your feeds and stories. And videos will be much more authentic and real-time.

With increasingly advanced mobile phone cameras, it's now incredibly easy to create a high-quality video spontaneously, and followers will be excited to see more and more authentic content.

In 2022, instead of posting a photo, we suggest you post a 3-10 second video of a specific moment and see what happens!

As of the end of 2019, Instagram has made a drastic change: You will no longer be able to see likes for published posts.

Instagram is still testing hidden Likes on accounts around the world. In many countries, such as Canada and Australia, public Likes have not been available for months.

The decision to hide Likes is largely due to the fight against mental health issues arising from the platform. Indeed, social media leads to feelings of anxiety, depression, low self-esteem, loneliness, and isolation for many users. This is particularly worrying for young users of the platform.

According to most marketers around the world, a second motivation for the decision to hide post likes would be to get people to post more in their feeds. Many creators, users, and brands have put more emphasis on Likes in recent years, which has led to a drop in annual feed posts.

Instagram users used to save only their best content for the feed to keep engagement rates high across all their posts.

But by removing likes, Instagram's theory is that people will be able to be more creative and post what they want without worrying about how many likes they will get for a post. If this is successful, Instagram is also likely to see an increase in post feeds.

Once Likes are permanently hidden, it's very likely we'll see a more dramatic change in visual content and an increase in feed posts.

Why are post feeds so important to Instagram? Since the explosion of Instagram Stories, more and more Instagram users are spending time looking at Stories rather than scrolling through their feeds, and that's where the biggest ad dollars are (ads on Stories are increasing, but because they're newer, they have more limited options and ad inventory).

What does all this mean for a marketer? Less time editing and more time creating content. You then have the opportunity to rethink your feed, with the flexibility to publish more content with fewer restrictions and see how your audience responds.

11. Don't underestimate TikTok.

You can't talk about Instagram in 2023 without talking about TikTok.

TikTok is a video-sharing app that typically focuses on music and is popular with young people (and now adults). TikTok's app was the third most downloaded app in 2019 and has about the same usage as Instagram Stories, with 500 million active users.

In 2023, you can expect TikTok to have a big impact on the type of content you'll see on Instagram, particularly Instagram Stories.

Why is TikTok being so successful?

For one, TikTok's content is incredibly real, unfiltered, and focused on content rather than aesthetics. For example, many of the videos are shot in the parents' basements homes rather than the well-lit living rooms of Instagram.

Furthermore, TikTok is a fun, if casual, platform, and incredibly popular for its ability to make your content go viral. At the heart of TikTok is the "For You" page, which is their version of Instagram's "Explore" tab and is an incredibly powerful engine for content distribution.

You can have 20 followers, create a video and get over 1 million views and thousands of followers!

So while Instagram is moving away from counting likes and its algorithm is making it harder for your content to be seen by your followers, TikTok offers marketers the exact opposite.

We'll be creating a lot more TikTok content in 2023, but when it comes to marketing the business and driving sales, Instagram is the best (and most challenging) platform to focus on.

Your goals for TikTok should focus solely on brand awareness, as you can't currently add a link to your TikTok bio!

Do you want to use Instagram effectively in your business or increase performance?
Instagram has become an extremely useful tool for all businesses, even small ones because it allows you to create an active and vibrant community without having to make a large investment.

This tool is an important and powerful way for anyone to reach a large audience at a relatively low cost. However, many of you who might be managing social media marketing activities for a small or medium-sized business know that it is not always easy to devote the right amount of time and energy to your Instagram account.
In discussions between various specialists in the many groups dedicated to Instagram marketing, and in constantly trying to figure out how to be as efficient and effective as possible, we have noticed three main weaknesses:
Planning and creating content takes time.

An effective account layout is one of the most important factors in growing your audience, but the process of constantly planning the look of our account grid and creating great content takes a lot of time and resources.
Keeping up with posting schedules daily often interrupts a marketer's workflow.

We all know it is important to post frequently and be consistent with posting schedules. The problem is that defining a way to remember when to post content and pausing everything several times a day to keep up with the schedule is a huge challenge for a daily workflow.

Constantly optimizing content to increase interaction is no easy task

As Instagram's algorithm is constantly changing, the evolution of the content presented to the audience is continuous. This evolution usually constantly reduces interaction rates, which has a negative impact on your business. The problem is that it is often not easy to identify what has changed and how best to adapt to these changes.

Building such a loyal and engaged community across multiple channels is never easy, but with the right approach and experimentation, you will find a solution tailored to your brand.

Not to mention generating new leads, customers, and sales.

CHAPTER 14

INSTAGRAM ADS 2023

You've probably read or heard about brands that have found success with Instagram Ads.

You might be thinking it's time to develop an Instagram advertising strategy for your business and wondering where to start.

What is Instagram Ads and how does it work? How much does it cost to advertise on Instagram? How do you create an effective campaign and sponsor a post or story? In this guide, I will try to answer all your questions.

What is Instagram Ads?

Instagram Ads is the social network's advertising "circuit" for sharing videos and photos.

When a brand wants to sponsor an ad or content on Instagram, they pay the platform to show the ad to a specific audience. Instagram often signals that it is an ad by adding the label 'Sponsored' to the post.

Instagram Ads: Sponsorship

Sponsored posts typically take the form of a carousel, slideshow, static image, or video.

They can also include a call-to-action - such as "buy now" or "learn more" - depending on the goal of the campaign, i.e. whether the sponsor wants to generate more traffic, increase followers on Instagram or increase conversions.

Instagram ads: Types of ads

If you want to advertise on Instagram, you can sponsor your content in different formats. These are some of the most interesting ones:
- Stories Ads
- Explore ads
- Collection Ads
- Shopping ads

Let's take a look at the details of each.

Ads in Stories

These ads are posted in Stories and take up the user's entire screen.

Instagram Ads: Story ad.

Sponsored stories have a call to action that encourages the user to "swipe up", i.e. scroll the screen from bottom to top to purchase a product or discover the offer.

Instagram Stories offers several tools to capture the audience's attention, such as video effects, facial filters, and stickers.

Ads in Explore

Instagram has a section called Explore where users can discover content related to their interests.

However, they do not see ads on this page, but only after opening a photo or video and scrolling down to see more 'like posts'.

Instagram Ads: Explore

The main advantage of ads in Explore is that you can run them at the same time as sponsored posts by selecting Explore as an additional placement (we'll go into more detail later).

Collected Ads

Collected ads allow users to view and purchase products on Instagram.

When they click on a product within the collection, they are redirected to Instant Experience (the social network's e-commerce platform).

Instagram ads: ads with a collection

These are creative sponsorships that typically include a collection of product images or videos.

Shoppable ads

You can also sponsor 'shoppable' photos and videos.

When the user clicks on the image, they are taken to an Instagram page with a description of the product. Clicking the "Show on website" button will take them directly to your online shop where they can complete their purchase.

Why advertise on Instagram?
Advertising on Instagram is an effective way to promote your products to a very wide audience.
With over 500 million users using the platform every day, you can target a large customer base.
Not to mention, engagement on Instagram is on the rise. This means that the response rate to your campaigns can be higher than on other social networks. Businesses using Instagram Ads can generate 4 times more interactions than on Facebook. In addition, 80% of Instagram users say they decided to make a purchase based on a post or story they saw on the app.

With Instagram Ads, you have the opportunity to highlight your business, promote your products directly in users' feeds and increase your shop's sales.
You can set up sponsorships on Instagram using Facebook Ads Manager, which offers advanced options and tools for targeting and budget optimization. If you've already managed Facebook Ads campaigns for your business, you'll have no trouble following this guide to ads on Instagram.

How much does it cost to advertise on Instagram Ads?
There is no universal answer to this question. However, I know from experience that the cost of ads on Instagram varies

depending on the destination, days of the week, demographics, ad placement and other factors.

For example, targeting a Millennial audience costs more than targeting an adult audience: users in the 25-34 age group are the most desirable on social media.

Because Instagram is busiest during the week, the cost of a sponsored ad is also higher on weekdays.

The placement of the ad also determines its cost: you will spend more to promote the content in users' feeds than other options. Again, AdEspresso reports that the average CPC for sponsored ads in multiple placements is $1.20 (€1.03).

When trying to calculate your campaign budget, ask yourself how much a conversion is worth to you and try to initially spend around $20-50 (€17-43). Then test everything and focus on the campaigns that get the best results. Use the Instagram Insights tool to measure the performance of your ads and invest a little more in those that increase engagement and sales.

How to create ads on Instagram

While Instagram doesn't give you the option to create ads directly within the platform, you do have two options. You can:

Sponsor posts you've made on Instagram in the past, or create ads using Facebook Ads Manager.

Let's start with the easiest one.

To sponsor a post on Instagram
The easiest way to start advertising on Instagram is to promote a post you've published in the past.
Select the post that has generated the most engagement and tap the 'Highlight' button in the bottom right-hand corner.

Advertising on Instagram
To do this, you need to have a business profile (also called a "business profile"). Only then will you see this option. If you have a personal profile, read this guide on creating or switching to a business profile.
Until recently, to advertise on Instagram, you also had to link Instagram Ads to a business Facebook page.
However, a few weeks ago the company announced that it would allow new advertisers in some countries to create sponsorships without having to link the account to a Facebook page.
So when you sponsor a post on Instagram for the first time, you can monitor and manage your campaigns directly on the platform.

How to create ads on Instagram with Facebook Ads Manager
Since Instagram and Facebook are closely linked, you can also use the Facebook Ads Manager to create ads on Instagram.
The Facebook Ads Manager is a powerful tool that allows you to customize your target audience down to the smallest detail.

You can also use it to define the objective of your campaign and monitor the performance of your ads.

To access Facebook Ads Manager, you need a Facebook account linked to a Facebook business page, to which you must also link your Instagram account.

Here's how:
1) Open your Facebook business page;
2) Go to Page settings > Instagram;
3) Click on the blue "Connect account" button;
4) Add your Instagram account details;
5) Click on "Save".

Once done, you can use Facebook Ads Manager to create ads on Instagram.

I guess that you are just starting and have never sponsored on Instagram or Facebook before. This is exactly what you need to do to create your first Instagram ad campaign.

1. Choose a target

To get started, open Facebook Ads Manager, click on "Ads Management" in the left-hand menu, and then click on the green "+ Create" button in the Campaigns tab.

Facebook ads manager new campaign

You can choose between the Create Wizard and then Quick Create. If you want detailed instructions on how to start a campaign on Instagram, select Create Wizard.

Facebook Ads Manager presents you with a list of goals in three categories.

Campaign goals

Think about the results you want to achieve: Do you want to generate more sales? Collect more leads? Increase brand awareness? Define the purpose of your campaign on Instagram and then choose the most appropriate option according to your needs.

Choosing the right target is crucial, as Facebook will determine which targets, formats, and placements are best for your ads based on your choices.

If you have an online shop, your main goal will probably be to increase sales. In this case, the most suitable option for your campaign is "conversions".

However, if you want to use Instagram Ads to drive more conversions, you still need to do one thing: generate a Facebook Pixel and install it in the backend of your online shop. This is a snippet of code that you need to put on your website to track conversions and sales.

If your shop is managed by Shopify, all you have to do is copy the pixel code from Facebook Ads Manager and paste it into the "Pixel ID" field in Shopify's settings.

With Facebook Ads Manager, you can also decide where to redirect users who click on your Instagram ads.

For example, you can send them to your online shop, an app, Messenger, or WhatsApp.

2. Give your campaign a name

Once you have selected your target, Facebook Ads Manager will ask you to give your campaign a name.

Although you can use generic names such as "Campaign 1", it's best to specify elements such as destinations, ad format, etc. This way you can immediately identify your target audience.

This way you can immediately identify the different campaigns and measure their performance more easily.

Campaign name

Now you can test your campaigns to see which strategy produces the best results.

By running A/B tests, Instagram compares different variables and allocates the biggest budget to the one that works best.

3. Define your budget and editorial plan.

Now you can define how much you want to spend on your campaign and how long it should last.

You have two options: You can select "Optimise campaign budget" or set it manually.

The "Optimise campaign budget" option is a new feature of Ads Manager. It identifies the best-performing adverts and allocates the budget to them, always taking into account your spending limits and the offer for each advert.

Optimize your ad campaign budget

If you have never used Instagram Ads before, I recommend selecting "Optimise campaign budget": this will allow you to spend as little as possible on each conversion.

In Facebook Ads Manager, you can also choose between a daily budget and a total budget. What they mean:

The daily budget refers to the average amount you want to spend per day on multiple ads or a campaign;
The total budget refers to the amount you want to spend for the duration of your ad or campaign.

If you decide on a total budget, you can also set up a specific plan for the publication of your ads.

Campaign budget
For example, you can set up your campaign so that ads on Instagram are only shown on weekends, or days and hours when your audience is most active.

4. Choose your target audience
This is where the fun begins.
You can now select all the characteristics of the audience you want to reach with your Instagram ads: demographics, interests, and behaviors.
For example, let's say you sell smartphones to millennials in Italy. Here you can select 'Italy' as the location and specify 'smartphone' and 'technology' as the interests in the corresponding fields.

On this screen, you can also create a customized target group. For example, you can target people who have visited your website. Or users who have already shopped in your shop and whose information you already have.

Well, now we can move on to ad placements (i.e. where they should appear and be seen by users in the app).

5. Selecting ad placements

Facebook Ads Manager gives you two options for placing your ads:

Automatic placements: If you select this option, Instagram will show your ads in multiple placements depending on where they perform best;

Manual placements: You can manually choose which platforms to show your ads on if you select this option.

To start sponsoring your ads, select "Manual placements" and tick the appropriate boxes on Instagram.

6. Create your first Instagram ad

Now all you have to do is choose a format, upload your content and write your ad text.

You can choose from several types and formats.

Choose the format that best suits your ad campaign on Instagram.

Upload an image or video that is relevant to your ad and add text in the caption field.

Note: Make sure you choose the right size because Ads Manager will not accept your ad if it is incorrect.

Creating Instagram Ads

Tip: Instagram offers several apps that allow you to create more effective images or videos for your ads. The layout is great because it allows you to combine several images into one photo. If you want to sponsor videos on Instagram, check out Hyperlapse, which allows you to create real-time videos while on the go.

If you've selected "Conversions" as your campaign objective, you'll also need to include call-to-action text. Choose the one that best suits your goals and audience.

When you're ready to launch the first sponsored post on Instagram for your business, click the green "Publish" button.

Conclusion

That's it. I hope you found this guide on Instagram Ads useful. Now you know what Instagram Ads are and how they work, how much it costs to advertise on Instagram, how to create ads and launch your first ad campaign.

Please note that advertising on Instagram is just the beginning. You also need to monitor the performance of your campaigns over time.

Even if you have planned and structured your campaigns down to the last detail, you must evaluate the results to see what you can improve and identify ways to reduce your spending.

For example, you may find that the conversion rate of one ad is 5 times higher than that of other campaigns. Or that a particular placement costs less.

The easiest way to measure the performance of your ads on Instagram is to use the analytics tool built into Facebook Ads Manager.

By monitoring your campaigns and using the data in reports, you can determine the best setting for each ad.

Printed in Great Britain
by Amazon

16027701R10092